Joyce R. Becker

Beautifully Embellished
Landscapes

125 Tips & Techniques to Create Stunning Quilts

C&T PUBLISHING

Text and Artwork © 2006 Joyce R. Becker
Artwork © 2006 C&T Publishing, Inc.

Publisher: *Amy Marson*
Editorial Director: *Gailen Runge*
Acquisitions Editor: *Jan Grigsby*
Editor: *Cyndy Lyle Rymer*
Technical Editors: *Nanette S. Zeller and Teresa Stroin*
Copyeditor/Proofreader: *Wordfirm, Inc.*
Cover Designer: *Kristen Yenche*
Design Director/Book Designer: *Rose Wright*
Illustrator: *Tim Manibusan*
Production Assistant: *Kiera Lofgreen*
Photography: *Diane Pedersen* and *Luke Mulks* unless otherwise noted
Scenic photography: *Valori Wells*

Published by C&T Publishing, Inc., P.O. Box 1456, Lafayette, CA 94549

Library of Congress Cataloging-in-Publication Data
Becker, Joyce R.
  Beautifully embellished landscapes : 125 tips & techniques to create stunning quilts / Joyce R. Becker.
     p. cm.
  Includes bibliographical references and index.
  ISBN-13: 978-1-57120-360-1 (paper trade)
  ISBN-10: 1-57120-360-5 (paper trade)
  1. Machine appliqué. 2. Machine quilting. 3. Quilts. 4. Fabric pictures.   5. Landscape in art. I. Title.
  TT779.B395 2006
  746.46'041--dc22   2006000761

Printed in China

10 9 8 7 6 5 4 3 2 1

Contents

Dedication

To my twin sister, Jan White—through it all, you continue to inspire everyone who knows and loves you, especially me!

To Patti, Rosy, and Denise—the best friends in the whole wide world!

To my parents, Ima Jo and Bill Burgreen—for believing in me.

Acknowledgments

My special thanks go to the incredible staff at C&T Publishing. You make me feel special and treat me so well. To my amazing editor, Cyndy Rymer, where would I be without you? To the rest of my team—Nanette Zeller, Kiera Lofgreen, and especially Diane Pedersen and Luke Mulks—thank you for your wisdom and continued guidance. To Amy Marson, Jan Grigsby, Mari Dreyer, Janet Levin, and the rest of the crew at C&T, thanks for believing in me. Without the stunning scenic shots, this book would be incomplete, so I thank Valori Wells for letting me share her incredible inspirational photographs.

To my handsome, well-loved husband, Donald, you are the best. Thank you for your support and love and for again proofreading my manuscript. To my stepdaughter, Bev Valdez, thank you again for your valued input and editing skills. To the rest of my family and cherished friends, thanks for being there for me and seeing me through yet another writing adventure. To my students and peers, thank you for your continued support. To the artists who contributed to this book, thank you for allowing me to showcase your spectacular art. To my friend and peer Jane Moxey, world-famous quilting television personality, thank you for your amazing expertise and advice. May you receive the recognition you truly deserve.

I firmly believe that God creates each of us with a special purpose in mind. I discovered that my purpose is making landscape quilts and sharing my techniques with others. Who would have thought that a freckle-faced adolescent struggling to pass "gathered skirts" in home economics would one day be traveling around the world teaching others to quilt? As a student of journalism, I figured I'd one day write smutty novels. But quilting books? What a hoot!

In my travels, I've noticed many students filled with anticipation, seeking more information and direction on how to make their magnificent landscape quilts shine with realism. Although my previous book about landscape quilting, *Luscious Landscapes*, provided the basics, this book dives into the really juicy stuff: the special effects and embellishments that make landscapes zing with realism. When it comes right down to it, creating realistic landscape quilts is more about problem solving than it is an artistic endeavor. I find myself asking, "How can I make a fence or barn look weathered or impart the mood of fog in the distance or create dancing sunbeams on the water?" Or "How can I transform or make the fabrics I have on hand mimic what I see in nature?"

Making Fabrics Your Own

Using my quilts and those of my students and peers as examples, I share insights with you on manipulating commercial fabrics, which I refer to as *making the fabrics your own.* Whether you transform fabrics using surface-design techniques, such as cutting, painting, machine embroidery, overlays, or shading, or you incorporate computer-generated clip art, the goal is the same: to recreate what you see in nature, using fabric as the medium.

There Are No Rules!

Traditional quilters often say that they find landscape quilting intimidating. As a quilter whose roots are steeped in traditionalism, I am here to tell you that creating landscape quilts is nonthreatening, freeing, and downright fun!

There are few rules, no seam allowances, and no pesky edges to turn. You don't need an art degree or any quilting experience. Some of my best students are beginning quilters! My landscape quilts are created purely from a love of nature, not from a background in art. I have no formal art background. In fact, the only real disagreement my husband and I ever had occurred while we were playing Pictionary: My drawing was so darn bad that he couldn't tell what I drew, and we lost the game!

I hope you'll enjoy the techniques and tips, the gorgeous landscape quilts, and the exceptional scenic photography by Valori Wells. After you learn new techniques and tricks to create landscape quilts, perhaps you'll jump in and try one of the projects. My ultimate wish for you is that you will be able to create an original landscape that sings with special effects and embellishments and that brings joy and happiness first to you and then to others.

CHAPTER ONE

Building Blocks

Why do landscape quilts evoke such feelings of calmness, well-being, and serenity? Nature-inspired landscape quilts remind us of places we've been, special memories, places we want to visit, or just places that take our breath away because they are so incredibly beautiful. Perhaps the tranquility of a peaceful landscape quilt offers us a momentary escape from the pressures of daily life.

Creating a successful landscape quilt is not difficult. With a good source of design inspiration and fabrics that do most of the work for you, you're well on your way. Using my surefire methods of "cut and glue" in combination with raw-edge appliqué, you can complete your quilt top in a matter of days, not weeks or months! You will be creating a landscape quilt with fabric as your medium, cutting and gluing fabrics to a stabilized muslin base, or "canvas." When your design is complete, you will baste the entire composition with invisible thread and then add the special effects and embellishments that will make your landscape come alive.

Detail of *Zack at Great Pond*, Cyndy Rymer, Danville, California, 46˝ × 31˝, 2005. Full quilt on page 65.

This photo provides good visual inspiration. (Photograph by Joyce R. Becker)

Where to Begin

With landscape quilts, your starting place is a visual inspiration. Original photographs, greeting cards, calendars, photography books, and even rough sketches are all suitable inspirations. Look for visual inspirations that have interest in the distance, the middle ground, and the foreground.

Once you have found your inspiration image, enlarge it to at least $8\frac{1}{2}$˝ × 11˝.

Photograph by Joyce R. Becker

Simplify

Look carefully at your visual inspiration. Can you eliminate something that seems unessential—what I refer to as "extra stuff"? Eliminating the trees on the right side of the photograph simplifies the design.

Copyright laws require that you obtain written permission from an artist before copying his or her work. It is appropriate to acknowledge or credit an artist who has inspired your work, particularly when you are entering your work into a competition.

Creating a Canvas

When designing a landscape quilt, you first need to create a "canvas." Cut a piece of muslin at least 4″ larger on all sides than the desired finished size (without borders) of your landscape quilt. The extra fabric around the perimeter allows for shrinkage from stitching and for squaring your quilt later on. Stabilize the back of your muslin canvas with Pellon fusible lightweight interfacing cut to the exact size of the muslin. To fuse the interfacing to the muslin, preheat your iron to a medium setting with steam. Place the fusible interfacing on a protected ironing surface, bumpy side up. Place the muslin on top of the interfacing and press.

It truly makes a huge difference which brand of fusible interfacing you use. Because of the weight and hand, Pellon brand is the only fusible interfacing that works with machine embroidery. An interfacing that is too dense will drag in your machine.

Stabilizer and muslin. Press with steam on medium setting.

If the fusible interfacing bubbles, your iron is too hot. You can reuse the interfacing, though. Simply wait for it to cool, peel it back, and reposition it. If the interfacing doesn't stick to the muslin, your iron is too cool.

Design Wall

A design wall is invaluable when you are designing your landscape quilt. Choose a spot in your studio or sewing room that will allow you to stand back and view your quilt as it progresses. If you don't have a design wall, there are inexpensive options. For example, a flannel-backed tablecloth or a piece of flannel or batting taped to a closet or blank wall can serve as a temporary design wall.

Designing on a flat surface such as a table will not provide the necessary perspective. Your quilt will be static or one-dimensional, and the finished product will never look quite right. If you are working on a foam-core board or another smaller surface, prop it up on a chair.

Selecting Fabrics

When you shop for fabrics for your landscape quilt, throw out all the "rules." Instead, begin thinking about what is most important—value and scale. Although color is always important in landscape quilts, value and scale are more important.

Value

Focus on and think about all that you see in nature. I know I do. When you see rows of mountains in the distance, for example, what do you notice? The lightest-value mountains are always in the distance, with medium-value mountains in the center, and the darkest mountains

Value is key when designing landscape quilts.

in the foreground. Creating this perspective in your landscapes is easy once you understand the logic. Think of yourself as a watercolor artist, painting a picturesque scene on your canvas. Your goal is to accomplish the same effect but with fabric as your medium. When you create rows of mountains on your canvas, color isn't as important as value. *The value of the fabrics, light to dark, creates the perspective.*

Scale

After value, the next most important consideration when selecting fabrics is scale. I positively love shopping for landscape fabrics for my quilts. I am constantly asking myself things like, "How can I use this fabric for tree bark? Does this fabric look like clusters of tree leaves? Does this fabric look like a thatched roof on a cottage?" Our job when selecting landscape fabrics is to *mimic what we see in our inspiration.* Keep in mind that the rule for scale is that objects in the foreground appear larger than objects in the distance. Once we select fabrics in the correct value and scale, we can manipulate them with surface-design and cutting techniques that make them resemble a variety of natural elements.

Fabrics love to be cut into! If you find a wonderful meadow fabric, but it has panda bears throughout, buy it anyway. You can cut away the panda bears and use them for another project.

It's All About the Fabric

I am often asked, "How do you know what will work and what won't work when shopping for appropriate landscape fabrics?" There is no magic formula for selecting landscape fabrics, but certain types of fabrics work well. Hand-dyed (see Resources) and hand-painted fabrics are heavenly and always blend well in landscape quilts, often doing half the work for you. Batiks look natural, but avoid those with large-scale directional motifs. Commercial fabrics printed with elements from nature such as pebbles and rocks, grasses and flowers, water and clouds, and so on are absolutely terrific.

When shopping for landscape fabrics, remember that you might be able to alter the fabric, or some element of it, either by cutting it smaller or by manipulating the value or color. Perhaps you are searching for a commercial print with bright red roses, but all that's available in the right scale is a print with bright pink roses. Buy it anyway! (See Chapter 3.)

Recolor commercial fabrics with inks or cut the motifs smaller.

Look at both sides of the fabric. Sometimes the "wrong" side of the fabric works better than the "right" side. Sometimes you will get lucky and be able to use both the front and the back of a fabric to create perspective.

Great Landscape Fabrics

Auditioning Your Fabrics

Once you've selected the fabrics for your landscape, it's time for the final test. Pin the fabrics you've selected onto your design wall. How do they look together? Does one fabric stick out like a sore thumb? Perhaps one fabric is too bright, or its value is too strong. Consider eliminating that fabric and substituting another. I find that following this simple formula helps when selecting fabrics for landscape quilts: *Put muddy colors with other muddy colors, and put clear colors with other clear colors.*

Let your fabrics hang on your design wall for a few days to "percolate." You might find yourself thinking about additional ways to use each fabric in your landscape. Sometimes, I think the fabrics actually speak to me if I let them hang around for a while on the design wall before I use them.

Audition fabrics on a design wall.

Tools

Today, most quilters have on hand almost everything they need to create landscape quilts. However, there are some specific products that I recommend.

Sewing Machine and Darning Feet

The most important piece of equipment you need for creating a landscape quilt is a sewing machine that allows you to lower the feed dogs so you can do free-motion work. If you are new to or apprehensive about free-motion stitching and in the market for a new sewing machine, investigate Bernina's Aurora 440QE sewing machine, which has a stitch regulator for free-motion quilting (see Resources). In addition to the sewing machine, you will need a free-motion, darning, or spring-loaded foot.

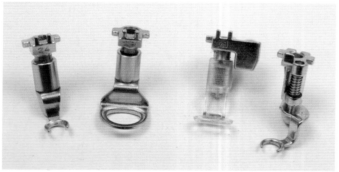

Free-motion feet

Scissors, Glue, and Starch

Next in importance is a good pair of razor-sharp scissors. I prefer large Fiskars Softouch scissors (see Resources). They are ergonomically correct and incredibly sharp, and they take a large bite of fabric when you cut, making cutting easier and more efficient. Of equal importance is a good-quality, repositionable spray adhesive, such as 505 Spray and Fix (see Resources), which you should be able to find at most sewing machine and quilt shops. If you wish, you may also use other types of spray adhesives, basting glues, or fabric glue sticks.

Another necessity is heavy-duty spray starch, which is available at grocery stores and drugstores. You can also mix up your own starch and place it in a spray bottle. Unfortunately, spray sizing just doesn't measure up to starch.

Threads and Rotary-Cutting Equipment

Other tools of importance include invisible thread; neutral or matching bobbin threads; rotary mats, rulers, and cutters; and lightweight Pellon fusible interfacing. Another helpful tool is a reducing glass or keyhole. When you stand back and look at your design through the reducing glass, it pulls all the elements together (see Resources).

Essential tools for landscape quilting

CHAPTER TWO

Enticing Techniques

Most landscapes include background elements, such as skies, mountains, grass, gardens, water, and so forth. Study your design inspiration and make a mental list of the background elements for your design. These elements are positioned and then glued onto your muslin canvas from the top of the quilt (e.g., sky) to the bottom (e.g., foreground). Look for wonderful hand-dyed or hand-painted fabrics or batiks for background fabrics. Avoid anything that has directional repeating motifs or patterns.

Avoid background fabrics with directional repeating motifs. The fabric on the left does not work; the fabric on the right does.

Building Your Background

Placement Guide

Once you've selected your fabrics and are ready to begin placing them on your muslin canvas, you will need a placement guide to tell you how much fabric to cut. Fold a copy of your $8\frac{1}{2}'' \times 11''$ (or larger) inspiration (photograph, drawing) in half horizontally. Fold it in half *again* horizontally. Using a pen or other marker, mark the fold lines on the outside edge of your enlarged inspiration. Repeat the process with your canvas.

Don't worry about the marks on your canvas; they will be hidden as your design progresses.

Fold and mark your inspiration and canvas.

How Much Fabric Do I Need?

Using the placement marks on your canvas and on your design inspiration, you can easily compute how much fabric to cut. Place your canvas on your design wall, with the design inspiration pinned next to it. The first step is to pin the sky fabric onto the canvas. Eyeball how much fabric you need, using the placement marks on your canvas as your guide. Cut the fabric, adding an extra inch or so as a precaution.

Building and Gluing Your Background Fabrics

After you cut the background sky, press it with steam until all the wrinkles disappear. The next step is to glue the sky onto the canvas.

Use an empty, clean, shallow box for gluing; otherwise, the spray adhesive will end up everywhere. Turn on a fan if you have one. If possible, it's a great idea to open the door for added ventilation. If the weather is nice, work outside. If you have any respiratory issues, wear a mask and spray the adhesive outside. Be sure to follow all cautions and warnings on the manufacturer's label.

Build Your Design From the Top Down

As mentioned earlier, it is best to build your design from the top (e.g. sky) down (e.g. foreground). Sometimes students get excited and want to jump to the foreground first. There is only one problem! Controlling the scale and perspective of your

Top (sky)

Down (foreground)

Build your landscape from the top down.

design is virtually impossible if you don't design from the top down. Lifting up already glued elements to tuck other elements into your design is difficult and often creates lumpy, uneven elements. Yes, there are exceptions, such as laying down a pathway, road, or river, but normally you start at the top and work down!

If you remember the fundamental art principle that it is *usually* lighter in the distance and darker in the foreground, the perspective in your landscape will occur naturally. Think about using both sides of your fabrics to differentiate value (lighter side in the distance, darker side in the foreground). Continue building your design from the top down until your design is complete.

This fabric could be used in the foreground (right side) and in the distance (wrong side).

Place the sky fabric right side down in a shallow box. Spray the fabric generously with adhesive, and then place it onto your canvas. If you don't like the placement, simply lift and reposition the fabric—that's the beauty of spray adhesive!

Place the fabric in a box right side down; spray liberally with adhesive.

If you end up with a background fabric that is too short, join two pieces together to make one complete background. Cut a curvy line on the inner edge of one piece, layer that piece on top of the second piece, and glue it into place.

Join two pieces of fabric to make one.

Continue building your background design. Audition, cut, press, and glue the remaining background fabrics onto your canvas in order, from the top of the quilt down.

Starch

As a quilter, I seek instant gratification. Anything that will make my job easier or quicker gets my vote of approval. Starch fits into that category. Starching makes cutting easier and keeps the raw edges from fraying. Before I cut into a fabric that will be used as an element in my landscape quilt (not including background fabrics), I starch it. Then I starch it again, then a third time. Count them up, partner—that's three applications of spray starch before the tips of my scissors hit the fabric! Don't starch large pieces of yardage; just starch enough fabric for your current needs.

When starching fabric, use a dry iron set on high. Let the starch soak into the fabric for about twenty seconds before pressing or you'll end up with little white flakes on your fabric. Keep a box of fabric softener sheets near your ironing board. If your iron becomes gummed up with excess starch, glue, or fusible materials, press your hot iron (cotton setting) on a fabric softener sheet. Use a scrap piece of fabric to protect your work surface. For stubborn areas, wad up a fabric softener sheet and scrub the hot iron directly. Be careful not to burn yourself, and keep in mind that acrylic nails will melt if they touch the hot iron.

Cutting 101

Once your background fabrics are in place, you will be cutting and gluing onto your canvas fabric pieces that mimic elements in nature. Your job is to translate what you see in your design inspiration by using fabric and scissors. *Mimicking these shapes is the single most important task when creating landscape quilts*. In addition to the basic shapes, consider the scale or size of the element. Before cutting a tree trunk, for example, audition the tree trunk fabric on your canvas to get an approximate size; use your inspiration and the placement lines as your guide. Think again before you get all choked up and say, "But I can't possibly cut a realistic tree!" This book makes it easy for you, and I furnish the tools you need. Chapter 5 provides specific cutting examples for many elements from nature, such as trees, mountains, waterfalls, and so on. Once you are adept at interpreting what you see when you cut into cloth, your landscape cutting will become second nature.

When cutting, *move the fabric, not the scissors*. Don't try this technique without starching the fabric first—it's virtually impossible.

Gluing Elements Into Place

If you are using a type of glue other than 505 spray adhesive, make sure you use enough to hold your elements in place until your piece is thread basted.

Spray adhesive tends to build up on your fingernails. Quilting expert Libby Lehman suggests keeping disposable packets of Goo Gone (see Resources) nearby to remove the glue from your fingernails. Also, storing your can of 505 spray adhesive upside down after use will keep the nozzle from gumming up and getting clogged.

Basting

Once you have layered and glued all the pieces onto your canvas, you need to baste the entire composition. Basting holds all the fabric bits in place on the canvas. The steps for machine basting your landscape design are as follows:

1. Lower the feed dogs on your sewing machine.
2. Use a darning or free-motion presser foot.
3. Insert an embroidery needle, size 75 or 90.
4. Thread your machine with clear or smoke-colored invisible thread. Depending on the values in your fabric, you may need to change thread colors during the process. Basting stitches will not be removed. For ease in threading, skip the last thread guide before the thread goes through the needle. Put the thread through the guide *after* the needle is threaded.

When you skip the last guide before the thread goes through the needle, the thread will not accidentally loop around the needle an extra time. This prevents thread breakage and skipped stitches and works for any type of sewing!

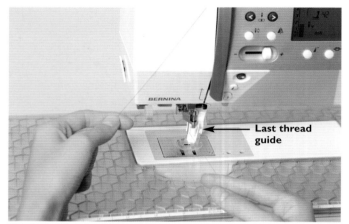

Skip the last thread guide.

5. Set the top tension on your machine so it is fairly loose— between 0 and 2 on most machines.

For most free-motion stitching, I put my thread in a wide-mouthed mug behind my machine. I lay the thread in the mug so it feeds off horizontally. Invisible thread, specialty embroidery thread, and quilting thread can be fickle. This step helps prevent the thread from jumping or breaking when you begin sewing.

The thread feeds horizontally from a mug.

6. Load your bobbin with a matching or neutral lightweight bobbin thread (see page 29).

7. "Walk" your bobbin to make sure your bobbin tension is correct. Place the bobbin in the case and hold the end of the thread; let the bobbin drop into your hand. If the thread feeds too quickly, tighten the screw on the case. If the thread doesn't walk, your tension is too tight, and you need to loosen the screw. Many machines with drop-in bobbins are self-adjusting.

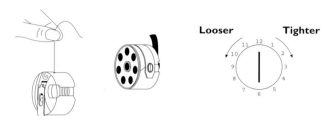

"Walk" your bobbin to test tension. Turn screw to adjust tension.

Many quilters keep an extra bobbin case just for free-motion stitching and leave the original bobbin case as is for normal sewing.

8. Carefully remove your landscape canvas from the design wall and place it under the presser foot. Unlike when quilting, you do not need to sew from the middle out when you are basting. I recommend basting the smallest elements to the canvas first.

9. To pull the bobbin thread to the top, insert the needle into the fabric with the presser foot down, then take the needle out of the fabric. Pick up the presser foot and pull up on the top thread. The bobbin thread should pop up to the top. Pull the loop gently until the thread comes through to the top. Put the presser foot down again and set your machine to the needle-down position. Take a few anchoring stitches and trim off the excess threads.

Some machines make an anchor stitch for you; others don't. If your machine doesn't have this feature, take a few stitches in place, trim the excess thread, and begin basting.

10. You control the canvas with your hands, "driving" or moving the fabric while you stitch around the outside perimeter of each element. There is no reason to stop and start and then cut threads during the basting phase. It is perfectly acceptable to "travel" (to stitch from one place to another). If you misjudge and stitch outside an

element, simply travel back to secure the edge. You don't have to be perfect when you baste. Your task is simply to secure the elements to the canvas.

Use your hands as an embroidery "hoop" as you move the fabric.

When traveling between elements during the basting process, stitch a curvy line rather than a straight one. The viewer's eye will be drawn right to a straight line.

Curvy basting line

Stitch a curvy line between elements.

Occasionally you may find that the edges of your elements have become unglued and stick up, making it difficult to baste. My solution is to slide a bamboo skewer under the darning foot and hold the edge of the fabric down with the skewer while you stitch. Your needle will skip over the tip of the skewer and usually won't break.

Use a bamboo skewer to hold edges down.

11. When you are finished basting, take a few anchoring stitches in place and then trim your threads.

Your basting is complete! You are ready to move on to the special effects and embellishments that will bring your landscape quilt to life.

CHAPTER THREE

Special Effects and Embellishments

This chapter and the next introduce you to the special effects and embellishments that will bring your landscape quilts to life. Creating the initial dynamic landscape design is fun and rewarding, but just wait until you experiment with the products and techniques I introduce to you! Your landscapes will zing with texture, dimension, and realism.

Quilters today are incredibly fortunate. The list of new supplies, fabrics, books, and other products created specifically for quilting grows longer each day. And it's my duty to try as many of the new products as I can to see how I can incorporate them into landscape quilts!

All-Purpose Inks

Among my newest discoveries are the all-purpose inks made by Tsukineko (see Resources). These inks are available in many colors and are applied with special applicators with round or pointed sponge tips. What makes these inks so irresistible? They are thin and fluid, much like airbrush paint. Rather than sitting on top of the fabric like textile paint, they are actually absorbed into the fabric like a dye. There is little or no migrating with these inks, and you can blend colors or use the inks with water as a wash (always pretest).

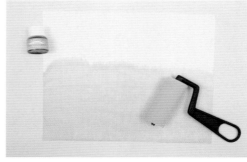

Dilute ink with water and use a sponge roller to create a color wash.

Create a flower with all-purpose inks and Fantastix applicators.

Change the color of a flower with ink.

Another way to use all-purpose inks to manipulate or modify commercial fabrics is demonstrated in *Covered Bridge* (full quilt on page 69). Pay particular attention to the rocks and the bridge.

Remember, *always* pretest the inks on a scrap of the fabric you are using to check the end result or to see whether adjustments are necessary. The only migration I have experienced with all-purpose inks has been on batik fabrics with a high thread count.

Commercial fabrics for the rocks and the bridge were enhanced with all-purpose inks.

When you apply all-purpose inks directly onto fabrics already stitched in place on your canvas, remember to place your landscape quilt top on a design wall to achieve the correct perspective. Place a piece of batting or a fabric scrap underneath the quilt top to protect your design wall. Apply inks from the top of the canvas down so you don't smear your work.

Stand back as you work to see whether you are getting the right effect. Looking through a reducing glass while standing back will help bring your landscape into the correct perspective, more like a finished product.

Heat Setting

All-purpose inks should be dried until tacky before they are heat set with an iron. It is perfectly acceptable to use a blow-dryer to speed up the drying process. Once the inks are dry, heat set each inked area without steam for about ten seconds. Place a pressing cloth or a piece of clean muslin on the quilt top before setting the all-purpose inks. (Tsukineko recommends letting each application dry before applying another color.)

Sponge tree bark using inks and a round-tipped applicator.

Netting, tulle, organza, and invisible threads melt with direct heat, so use a pressing cloth or press from the back. If you heat set from the back, a pressing cloth is not necessary, unless you've used invisible thread in the bobbin.

If you forget the heat-setting step, the all-purpose inks may run when they come in contact with water or steam from the iron. Having made this mistake myself, I strongly advise you to heat set your inks as soon as they are dry. Don't wait!

Textile Paints

Incorporating textile paints (see Resources) into your landscape quilts is another method of manipulating fabric to make it your own. If you find a fabric that is perfect for your landscape quilt but the color is wrong, consider using textile paint to transform the fabric. When I created *Cabin in the Woods* (full quilt on page 76), I wanted a sparkly grayish fabric for the frozen stream. To get the desired color, I painted a greenish sparkly fabric that was the correct value, but the wrong color, with a mixture of white and gray textile paints, thinned with a small amount of water.

This is stream fabric before and after painting

Applying textile paint does change the hand, or feel, of the fabric. The fabric will be slightly stiffer where the textile paint has been applied.

Highlighting is another trick you can incorporate. For example, in *Safe Harbor* (full quilt on page 63), I highlighted the water hitting the shore with white opaque textile paint to make the water look more realistic.

To add definition and interest, highlight the shoreline with textile paint.

Textile paints can also be used to create the appearance of sunlight reflecting on water, as demonstrated in *Reflections* (full quilt on page 61).

Create water reflections with textile paints.

There are several methods for applying textile paint: paintbrushes, sponge rollers, sponge brushes, sea sponges, or toothbrush splatter. Be creative. Think about what you want to accomplish. When you use paints, inks, fabric pens, or paint sticks, you are problem solving in an effort to make your landscape look realistic.

Dry your textile paints with a blow-dryer to avoid smudges or smears on your precious landscape quilt. Hold the blow-dryer about 8˝ away from your landscape quilt. Remember, you must heat set your textile paints with a *dry* iron and pressing cloth. NO STEAM!

In *Aloha Spirit* (full quilt on page 62), I painted the waves directly onto the water using white opaque textile paint and a medium artist paintbrush. After the paint was dry, I added white pearl textile paint to highlight the waves.

Try painting breaking waves with opaque white and white pearl textile paints.

When painting directly onto a quilt top, it helps to surround yourself with visual images as sources of inspiration and direction. When creating *Aloha Spirit,* I surrounded myself with several photography books to provide visual clues while I painted.

Fabric Markers

If you haven't used fabric markers on a quilt, perhaps it's time you gave them a try. It's amazing how much you can accomplish with these inexpensive little tools. For everything

Fabric markers are totally cool!

from shading to actually changing colors of elements, fabric markers are fantastic! Long gone are the inefficient fabric pens of yesteryear that dried up quickly and were often blotchy. Today's fabric markers are longer lasting and often have two tip options.

Fabric markers added shading in *Pernstejn* (full quilt on page 56).

My favorite brand of fabric marker is Fabrico by Tsukineko (see Resources). With fabric markers, you can add shading, change the color of an element, or enhance or deepen a value. You can even blend colors, if necessary, to create the correct color or value. Follow the specific instructions included with your markers. Not all fabric markers require heat setting.

When I created *Caleb, Waiting for the Cows to Come Home* (full quilt on page 58), I made the small flowers on the meadow grass with a yellow fabric marker to make the flowers pop. I changed the fence dramatically by adding long strokes with a brown fabric marker to give the fence more realism and dimension. I used the same marker to add small twigs and branches on the tree.

Fabric markers add realism.

Aloha Spirit (full quilt on page 62) offers another exciting example of how you can change colors and add shading using fabric markers. Take a look at the original palm tree. The fabric was a loose-weave, flimsy fabric. I began by starching the fabric several times, front and back. Once the fabric was starched, I shaded the tree and changed the values with fabric markers and thread. Compare the original palm tree fabric with the finished palm tree.

Here is the original commercial palm tree fabric; On the right is the tree fabric after it was enhanced with fabric markers and thread.

Artist Colored Pencils

Artist-quality soft-lead Prismacolor colored pencils are available at most art supply stores and on the Internet (see Resources). The soft lead in the Prismacolor pencils is permanent and water resistant. Although the intensity of the color is not as dramatic as that of fabric markers, the pencils come in a large variety of colors and can be blended. My well-used set of colored pencils includes 48 colors.

Compare the original flower with the flower colored with an artist pencil.

Artist pencils are particularly useful when your goal is subtle shading. In *Black Beach* (full quilt on page 80), for example, I printed an original digital photograph on fabric and subtly enhanced the colors in the water with colored pencils.

I shaded the water with Prismacolor colored pencils.

Another option is Derwent watercolor pencils. These water-soluble pencils can be used on dry fabric, like a conventional colored pencil, or with water. The pencils can also be used as a wash using a wet brush or wet fabric.

Shiva Artist's Paintstiks

Although Shiva Artist's Paintstiks look like giant crayons, they are real oil paints in a solid form (see Resources). Unlike other media described in this chapter, these paints require that you prewash your fabrics to remove any sizing. You can blend the Paintstiks, if desired. The paint is permanent once it has cured, or dried, for three to four days. After the paint has cured, it needs to be heat set. Place a piece of waxed paper over the area and heat set on medium high heat without steam for about ten seconds.

With Paintstiks, you can color directly on the fabric or change the color, value, or hue of a fabric, or you can stencil or stamp. Simply peel the protective film off the tip of the

Paintstik and sharpen if necessary; hold the Paintstik as you would a pencil (at an angle) and press to get the desired effect. Pretest on a piece of similar fabric before you incorporate the oil paint into your landscape quilt.

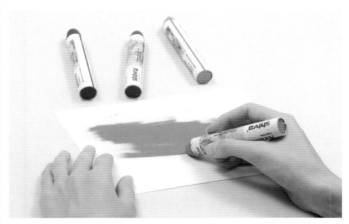

Shiva Artist's Paintstiks are oil paints in a solid form.

When stenciling with Paintstiks, determine where you want your stencil, spray the underside of the stencil with 505 spray adhesive, and press the stencil into place, making sure it lies flat and even. Rub the Paintstik directly onto a paper plate palette, pick up the paint with a stencil brush, and apply the color.

Rosy Carolan combined stenciling and painting in her landscape quilt *Summer Sizzle* (full quilt on page 86). She shaded part of the foliage with a green Paintstik and stenciled over the top using a stencil and a Paintstik. The stenciled portion of the quilt adds a traditional flair to the contemporary landscape quilt.

Detail of *Summer Sizzle* by Rosellen Carolan, full quilt on page 86.

Rubber Stamps

Scrapbooking and rubber stamping are all the rage with crafters today, and as a result, there are a large variety of rubber stamps available. Rubber stamps are not just for scrapbooking and can add wonderful detail to your landscape quilts. For example, in *Reflections* (full quilt on page 61), I used a rubber stamp and fabric stamp pad to stamp the tree boughs on the upper right side of the quilt. If your drawing talents are limited, rubber stamping helps accomplish realism in landscape quilts.

Rubber stamp and Tsukineko fabric stamp pad used in **Reflections.**
Use a padded surface and press straight down.

Always pretest your stamp and pad on a similar piece of fabric. Use a padded surface to stamp on, and don't wiggle your hand—press straight down and then lift the stamp straight up.

Boughs were stamped directly onto the quilt top.

I also used this method to create the tree boughs on the Douglas fir tree in *Safe Harbor* (full quilt on page 63). I stamped on a stabilizer, stitched over the stamped image with a heavy thread, removed the stabilizer, and appliquéd the boughs to the quilt top. Chapter 4 provides specific details on stabilizing, stamping, and embroidering techniques to build boughs of two kinds of fir trees.

Printing on Fabric

If you can print an image on paper, you can print it on fabric and incorporate it into your landscape quilt—choose from digital camera images and scanned original photographs, copyright-free images from books and computer programs, and images from the Internet. In today's high-tech environment, it's easy to "borrow" photographs or drawings from copyright-free sources for your landscape quilts.

If, like me, you are artistically challenged when it comes to drawing elements to include in your landscape quilts, clip art is an option for you. Greeting-card programs, such as Sierra Print Artist, PrintShop, Art Explosion, PrintMaster, and so on, are perfect. There are also copyright-free clip art and photographs available on the Internet, just waiting to be printed on pre-treated computer fabric sheets that you can send through your inkjet printer. Another great source for copyright-free images is Dover's series of clip-art books and CDs (see, for example, *Trees & Leaves* in the Bibliography).

If the thought of printing on fabrics seems intimidating, read *Photo Fun* and *More Photo Fun* (see Bibliography). These books take you step-by-step through each process. I've been incorporating computer images printed on fabric into my landscape quilts for years, and so can you.

Computer Fabrics

The choices for pretreated computer fabrics have improved dramatically. Quilt shops now stock pretreated computer fabric sheets in a variety of fabric options, including cotton and silk (see Resources).

There's a wide variety of choices for printing images onto pretreated computer fabric.

Each manufacturer has specific directions for printing—follow the directions *exactly.* If you skip a step, it's possible your image will bleed. Inkjet printers are recommended for printing on most fabric sheets. I use a Hewlett-Packard all-in-one inkjet printer.

A less expensive option is to make your own fabric sheets by soaking fabric in a fixative, such as Bubble Jet Set 2000 (see Resources). After soaking the fabric, let it dry and then iron it to remove the wrinkles. Reinforce the fabric by ironing freezer paper or a stabilizer on the wrong side so the fabric is stable enough to run through the printer. Again, check the manufacturer's directions.

Incorporating Images Into Landscapes Using a Copy Machine

If you have a great photograph or image but don't know how to begin, the first step is to determine whether the image is the right size. Use a copy machine to determine whether you need to enlarge or reduce the image. Print samples on computer paper first, audition them on your canvas, then adjust the size, color intensity, and dark/light contrast as necessary. The next step is to print the image directly onto pre-treated computer fabric (follow the manufacturer's directions).

Incorporating Digital Photographs Into Landscapes Using a Computer

In *Caleb, Waiting for the Cows to Come Home* (full quilt on page 58), I posed and shot a digital photograph of Caleb, my grandson.

Photograph of Caleb printed on pretreated computer fabric

I opened the photograph of Caleb in a photo-editing program that came with my digital camera (Adobe PhotoDeluxe, Business Edition; see Resources) and made adjustments as necessary. First, I reduced the size of the photograph, and then I printed it on computer paper. Once I had the desired size, I cut out the image and auditioned it directly on my quilt top to check the size. Next, I played with the intensity of the color and the brightness, so there would be more contrast. Finally, I printed images of Caleb using different settings and fabrics. In the printer options, I select normal paper rather than specialty paper, because the resulting image is typically brighter and truer.

I created *Bellows Beach* (full quilt on page 83) from an original digital photograph. With a good digital camera and a little imagination, you can set up a picturesque scene and make a quick-and-easy landscape quilt in nothing flat.

I created ***Bellows Beach*** from a digital photograph.

When taking digital photographs of landscapes, think about visual interest. Frame your shot the same way you would design a landscape quilt. Make sure there is visual interest in the background, middle ground, and foreground. There should be some negative space so the scene is restful and not too busy (negative space refers to the empty areas or background areas, such as the sky or water). Place the focus or central item on one side or the other, not in the middle.

Cow photographs came from a copyright-free site on the Internet.

Printing Photos on Fabric

Once you've determined the image you would like to use, you will need to crop, trim, and resize the image to fit your quilt. You may find it necessary to adjust color intensity, contrast, saturation, or hue. Choose a print resolution that is 150 dpi (dots per inch) or higher. Always print a trial copy on computer paper to test image quality and color intensity. Adjust the image again, if necessary. Print the image on pretreated computer fabric, following the manufacturer's directions. Select the normal or plain-paper option when printing.

Since all computers, digital cameras, scanners, and photo-editing software operate differently, please consult your user's manual or the software's Help menu for specific details about altering and saving your digital artwork.

Computer-Generated Clip Art and Photographs

As mentioned earlier, incorporating computer-generated clip art or photographs (see Resources), as long as they are copyright-free, is another option for printing directly on fabric. The photographs of the cows featured in *Caleb, Waiting for the Cows to Come Home* (full quilt on page 58) were downloaded from the Internet.

Searching for Copyright-Free Clip Art and Photographs

Use your favorite search engine and type in the appropriate keywords in the search box, for example, "copyright-free photographs (or clip art) of cows." The search engine Google seems to offer many options when it comes to copyright-free clip art and photographs. Other helpful search engines include Yahoo, AltaVista, dmoz, MSN, and Dogpile. Save the images and edit them in your photo-editing software.

Scanning Art

A scanner is also a good tool for generating images for landscape quilts. Perhaps you have a snapshot of a terrific scene you'd like to use in a miniature landscape quilt. Scanning is much like making a photocopy. Once you have scanned an image, you can edit it with your photo-editing software.

You can scan almost anything—children's artwork, fabric, flowers, buttons, ribbons. Scanned items printed on computer fabric can be incorporated into landscape quilts as focal points, borders, labels, and so on. What about a memory quilt, with houses or scenes from childhood homes, family camping outings, or all the wonderful places you have visited in your lifetime? Or scan photographs of your pets and create a poignant pet quilt. The list is endless.

CHAPTER FOUR

Fabulous Fibers and Tempting Threads

Part of my philosophy in life is to experiment, play, have fun, and share the talents entrusted to me. So it seems only natural that I also experiment when creating landscape quilts. I adore trying new techniques, some original, some not; some successful, some not! In this chapter, I'll share techniques that have worked for me and that you might enjoy including in your landscape quilts.

Fabulous Fibers

Overlays

One of my favorite techniques when creating landscape quilts is to incorporate *overlays*. Overlays can be sheer fabrics that you layer over portions of your landscape quilt to create distance or mood. Overlays can also be other fibers that add texture and dimension.

TULLE

Tulle is a fine-grade netting, often referred to as "bridal illusion tulle." Tulle is readily available at most large fabric shops, usually in a variety of colors. Some fabric shops also stock shiny or iridescent tulle or tulles sprinkled with motifs.

Although slightly more expensive than netting, tulle is often a better choice for landscape quilts because of its tighter weave. In *Cabin in the Woods* (full quilt on page 76), I added a layer of white tulle over the entire quilt top to give it a frosty appearance. Using overlays of tulle allows you to create subtle value changes easily. You can place several layers of tulle in your landscape quilts or even layer a variety of colors, one on top of the other.

Perhaps your landscape quilt just doesn't seem to blend together when it is complete. Maybe some of the separate elements jump out at you. Consider adding a single layer of tulle in a complementary color over the entire top. It will pull your design together and make it cohesive. In *Reflections* (full quilt on page 61), I placed a layer of white tulle over the entire top to make the piece flow together. The three-dimensional foliage in the foreground was added after the overlay of tulle. Think about using other colors for overlays as well. A layer of brown or black tulle in a fall scene can really make the colors pop while making the piece more unified.

Watch the advertisements. Fabric shops occasionally put tulle on sale for half price. I buy a yard each of at least ten colors when there is a sale. Storing tulle and other overlays is another story. Tulle competes with Houdini when it comes to being an escape artist. I have found that a large plastic bin with a lid works best.

Tulle comes in a variety of colors.

Tulle helps with consistency.

NETTING

Netting is stiffer than tulle, has a looser weave, and comes in a large array of colors. If you are unsure which colors of netting to buy, invest in a palette of blues and blue-greens. Netting is perfect for water overlays; it makes the water look slippery!

Netting and tulle can be combined as overlays as well, as demonstrated in *Aloha Spirit* (full quilt on page 62).

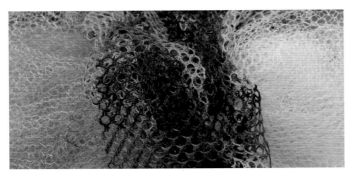

Netting has a looser weave than tulle.

A layer of turquoise *netting* was applied over the water; the deeper water has two layers of royal blue *tulle*.

ORGANZA

Organza is another sheer fabric that works well as an overlay. Although organza is available in silk and polyester, my pocketbook dictates polyester organza. Available in many colors, polyester organza comes in both matte and shiny finishes. Organza overlays are magic—they soften the appearance of fabrics that might be just a touch too strong in value; they also create the illusion of distance. As with tulle and netting, you can place several layers of organza on top of one another for shading or muting.

Polyester organza is available in a large variety of colors.

ANGELINA FIBERS

Like a kid in a candy store, I went wild when I discovered Angelina fibers and selected almost every color marketed. Angelina is a wonderful product. Made of loose polyester fibers, Angelina is available in a large range of colors that are both sparkling and iridescent. These fibers can be shredded, blended together, or used separately. The versatility of this product makes it highly desirable for textiles and landscape quilts.

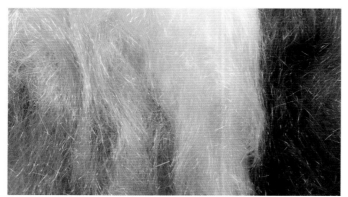

Angelina fibers come in a variety of colors.

Angelina comes in both an iridescent "hot fix" bondable variety and a nonfusible variety. I recommend the bondable Angelina for landscape quilting. Take a look at *Bellows Beach* (full quilt on page 83) and notice the iridescent glow of the water.

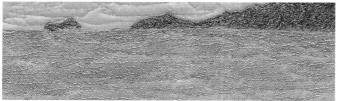

Create an iridescent glow with a layer of bonded Angelina fibers.

The possibilities for Angelina are endless. Think about Angelina in waterfalls, for waves hitting a beach, or for shimmering clouds in the sky. The illusion of ice on a frosty surface is evident in *Cabin in the Woods* (full quilt on page 76).

Angelina can be painted, shaped, contoured, or cut into tiny pieces and bonded onto other fabrics and then glorified with stitching. My advice is to play, have fun, and experiment. If you'd like more information about ordering Angelina, or if you'd like a reference book that spells out its myriad uses, check Resources (page 93) and Bibliography (page 94).

Try using Angelina fibers on snow.

TECHNIQUES FOR APPLYING OVERLAYS

The easiest method of applying an overlay of tulle, netting, or organza onto your landscape quilt is to add it during the design process. For example, after I glued the mountain shapes onto the canvas in *Covered Bridge* (full quilt on page 69), I extended a layer of white tulle over the top and bottom edges of the mountains. I pinned the tulle in place and continued building my design *on top* of the tulle. Later, when I basted my design with invisible thread, I stitched along the top edge of the mountains and cut away the excess tulle.

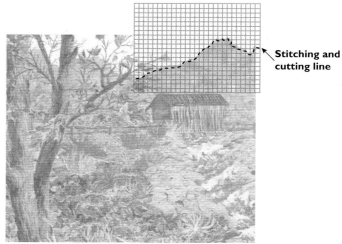

Stitching and cutting line

Stitch, then trim the tulle.

It is next to impossible to glue tulle, netting, or organza. Pin it into place carefully instead. All of these overlays have a mind of their own and like to shift and move while you are trying to stitch them into place. Use your hands to smooth the overlays into place as you stitch, watching out for sharp pins.

Applying Angelina is a whole different ball game. Basically, you produce your own nonwoven fabric from Angelina fibers. Simply shred the Angelina and arrange the color(s) as desired on tissue or parchment paper, cover with another layer of paper, and fuse following the manufacturer's directions. If you don't have parchment paper, computer or tissue paper works just fine. You end up with something that looks like a sparkling, colored dryer sheet! It's fun to experiment and blend more than one color of Angelina before fusing.

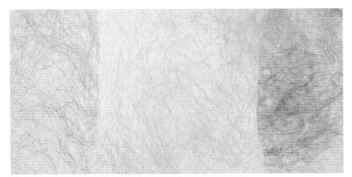
This is an example of bonded Angelina fibers.

Once you have produced your fabric sheet with the Angelina fibers, glue it to the surface of your landscape quilt using repositionable spray adhesive; then baste it into place with invisible thread. Later, during the machine-embroidery stage, consider using a matching thread to enhance the vibrancy of the Angelina.

When fusing Angelina fibers, if your iron is too hot you will end up with a melted nonwoven fiber sandwich without much sheen. Do a heat test first, using a small amount of Angelina. Timing can be tricky. I find that just touching the paper with the iron and immediately lifting the iron off the parchment paper provides plenty of heat to bond the fibers together without losing the sheen.

Batting and Dryer Lint

Batting is another great fiber that can be used in a variety of ways when designing your landscape quilts. Shredded or pulled apart, a low-loft batting can be used to enhance your landscapes. Look at the line of white at the water's edge in *Old World Charm* (full quilt on page 74).

Batting fibers couched next to the water's edge

I shredded a thin layer of low-loft Thermore batting around the edge of the water and couched (zigzag stitched) it into place with invisible thread. Think about using shredded batting in your landscapes to imitate subtle waves or waterfalls, or use it as snow.

In some circles, I'm known as the bag lady of dryer lint. My friends (and even some of their friends) faithfully save their dryer lint for me because when I teach, I demonstrate how to incorporate dryer lint into mountain scenes. Think about snow-covered mountains with outcroppings of wind-blown rocks. Why cut out all of those teensy tiny little rocks from commercial fabric if dryer lint will suffice?

I used dryer lint to create the rocky outcroppings on the mountain in *Safe Harbor* (full quilt on page 63).

TECHNIQUES FOR ADDING BATTING AND DRYER LINT

Batting should be applied to your landscape quilt during the design process. If the batting needs to be shredded, pull it apart *gently,* a little at a time.

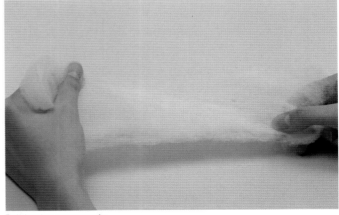
Pull batting apart gently.

After you pull the batting apart, mold it into place and pin it until you baste. The batting should either be stitched into place during the basting process or couched into place with invisible thread. If desired, cover the batting with a layer of tulle, which helps hold it in place.

Forget trying to glue your batting into place. You'll end up with a sticky, gluey mess with shreds of cotton batting sticking to your fingers instead of to your canvas!

I used green dryer lint to mimic moss.

Dryer lint positively loves to stick to commercial fabrics; just put it into place, thin it with your fingernails or a stiletto, and voilà, you have lovely, realistic outcroppings of rocks on your snow-covered peaks! In *Moods of Summer* (full quilt on page 66), I incorporated clumps of green dryer lint to look like moss. I stitched over the moss with a matching thread.

When creating rock outcroppings on mountains, you sometimes have to add a layer of netting or organza to hold the dryer lint in place. After placing the overlay of netting or organza over the dryer lint, baste the rocks with invisible thread and then add machine embroidery with matching threads on top of your outcroppings for a terrific dimensional mountain.

Tempting Threads

I can't say enough about the versatility and importance of threadwork and machine embroidery in your landscape quilts. Thread has the magical ability to transform your flat landscape into a complex piece, exuding texture and dimension. Threadwork draws the eye of the viewer into the quilt, practically begging you to notice the details. Imagine the bark on a Douglas fir tree. What would it feel like if you put your cheek to the bark? Would it be rough like sandpaper or smooth as silk? Now ask yourself how you can translate the roughness of the bark with thread.

The list of uses for thread on landscape quilts is endless. You can easily incorporate directional flow, detail, and textures with thread. Bear in mind that thread is your friend when you are creating elements that are too small to cut from fabric, such as branches or twigs on a tree, tendrils on a vine, the veins on a leaf, or crackling plaster on a garden wall or cottage.

Picture yourself on a tropical island on the beach. Can you see the sunlight dancing on the water and the waves rolling in and crashing on the shore? I created the directional flow of the water and the sparkling sunlight in *Aloha Spirit* (full quilt on page 62) with thread.

Thread creates directional flow and sunlight dancing on the water.

"I'm So Confused … What Type of Thread Do I Use?"

When asked what brand of thread I use, I shrug and reply, "Any brand that is the right value and color." I am not a purist. I will use almost *any* type of thread, from cotton to polyester to silk. However, I *don't* use rayon threads, mainly because they tangle easily and because I don't care for the unnatural sheen they add to my realistic landscape quilts. I am terribly conscious of when and where to use holographic, metallic, and sliver threads. I use those types of threads only if the quilt demands it. For example, in *Aloha Spirit* I used a holographic blue thread by Superior to impart the dancing sunlight on the water. For water and icy surfaces, sparkling thread is perfect. Most of the time, however, I prefer a standard 40-weight thread in either polyester or cotton. Whether the thread is from Superior, Sulky, Madeira, Isacord, Robison-Anton, YLI, or Coats & Clark (see Resources), what I look for is the correct value and color. I will admit, however, that my favorite brand of thread is Superior.

Let's discuss why you are able to use a wider variety of threads when you machine embroider as opposed to when you machine quilt. Typically, you use the same weight thread on the top and bottom when you machine quilt; otherwise, you are likely to encounter thread nightmares. When you machine embroider on a *quilt top,* however, you can use a heavy thread through the needle and a lightweight thread in the bobbin. The lightweight bobbin thread does not compete with the thread you use through the needle. It is possible to use a 30-weight or even a 12-weight cotton thread through a topstitch needle when you are machine embroidering on a quilt top. The thicker thread covers more space in less time and adds another level of texture. However, if you attempt to use a 30- or 12-weight cotton thread in both the needle and in the bobbin, you will, in all likelihood, end up with a nest of thread on the back. Also, the thread might break, or the needle could jam or break (see Bobbin Thread, page 29).

Specific brands of threads include different varieties, such as variegated and UltraTwist threads. Variegated threads, in the correct values and colors, do much of the work for us, adding wonderful subtle value changes that impart realism and texture. Instead of wide variations in value, Superior has recently introduced Rainbows variegated threads, which are closer in value, with 1″ color change intervals. Blendables, by Sulky, have random subtle color changes every 2.5″ to 5″ and come in 30- and 12-weight varieties. UltraTwist thread, also by Sulky, combines two colors of thread twisted together, creating "instant" texture in landscape quilts. (See Resources for Sulky and Superior threads.)

Specific varieties of threads add another dimension to landscape quilts.

Bobbin Thread

Before we discuss the actual techniques of machine embroidery, let's discuss bobbin thread choices. Bobbin thread is usually a thinner weight than top thread, typically a 60-weight thread. I *almost always* use a lightweight bobbin thread when I am doing any type of machine embroidery. There are many brands of bobbin threads available. Superior markets The Bottom Line, a lint-free filament polyester thread designed by quilt artist Libby Lehman and available in 50 colors. This thread is an exceptional choice, because it allows you to match the bobbin color with the top thread. It also doubles as an appliqué thread, if desired.

The Bottom Line bobbin threads by Superior

As most of you probably know, one little "dot" of bobbin thread always pops to the top. If we use a bobbin thread that closely matches the top thread, this dot goes unnoticed!

Other recommended bobbin threads include YLI Lingerie, as well as Bobbin Thread and Metrolene by Mettler. If you are unable to purchase matching bobbin threads, use a neutral bobbin thread, such as a gray or beige. Gray and beige bobbin threads blend with most fabrics, whereas white or black bobbin thread is easily noticed.

Where, How, and When to Machine Embroider

Machine embroidery or threadwork is executed when the quilt is still a top, *not* during the machine-quilting stage after the quilt is sandwiched.

Before you began designing your landscape quilt, you stabilized your muslin canvas (see Chapter 1). A stabilized canvas makes it easier to control and manipulate the quilt top as you stitch, because it doesn't get sucked down into the feed dogs. The stabilization step also helps prevent your landscape quilt from stretching out of shape. If you don't stabilize your canvas, you can expect some pretty hairy thread nightmares along the way. What do I mean by thread nightmares? Nests of tangled threads on the back of your quilt top, or worse, broken needles and jammed bobbins, coupled with a pounding headache! My advice is *always stabilize* your fabric and pretest your threads on a sample of fabric before you begin stitching on the quilt top.

This quilt demonstrates a wide variety of machine-embroidery stitching.

Where you start your machine embroidery on your quilt top isn't really important. You don't need to start in the middle and work out. What's most important is that you stitch all the elements that use the same thread color at the same time. Why? So you don't waste time changing threads. Perhaps it will ease some concerns if I lead you, step-by-step, through the machine-embroidery threadwork that I used on *Aloha Spirit*.

This machine-embroidery process demonstrates the types of stitching, the density of stitching, and the types of threads, as well as how machine embroidery enhances landscape quilts.

---

1. I incorporated many types of machine embroidery in *Aloha Spirit* to enhance the individual elements in the design. From the motion and directional flow of the waves, the seashore, the mountains, and palm tree fronds to the flowers and foliage, each element requires its own specific type of stitching. As seen previously, the stitching for the water is done with a sparkly, holographic thread.

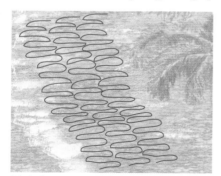

Stitch the movement of the water with blue holographic Superior thread.

2. To demonstrate the importance of value changes with thread, let's take a look at the different thread values that I used in the foliage and at the stitching pattern. Notice the different colors and values of thread and how my stitches follow the shape of the vegetation.

Notice the different thread colors and values.

Follow the shape of the bush when you machine embroider.

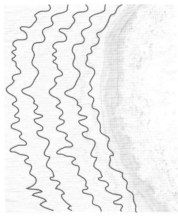

Stitch rows using a free-motion zigzag stitch, with the feed dogs down.

3. Now let's take a look at the detailed stitching in the sand. My goal was to impart how sand really looks after the waves have pulled back, so I free-motion quilted curvy lines using a matching thread and a zigzag stitch.

4. I did the stitching in the mountains with a matching variegated thread. I simply followed the crevices and contours of the mountains, trying to capture the correct directional flow, imitating the actual form of mountains in Hawaii.

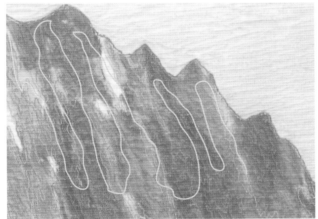

Follow the directional flow of the mountains.

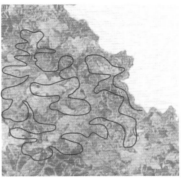

Use a stipple stitch in the foliage.

5. I used a stipple-type machine-embroidery stitch with a Sulky UltraTwist thread in the green foliage bordering the sand, giving more texture to the undergrowth.

6. In this quilt, the sky is not the focal point, so it needed to recede into the background. I used a matching blue thread and an elongated stitch.

Use an elongated stitch in the sky.

7. The palm tree, however, is the focal point of this landscape quilt. Although the tree has multiple treatments of all-purpose inks, fabric markers, and so on, what really brings the palm fronds to life is the machine embroidery. The shading on this palm tree was accomplished by machine embroidery using a thick, 30-weight Sulky dark green cotton thread combined with a shimmering golden and medium green polyester Sulky thread. When I appliquéd the palm tree fronds onto the canvas, I extended the machine embroidery on the shaggy palm fronds with threads.

Enhance the palm tree with dense machine embroidery.

Extend the machine embroidery to make the palm fronds look shaggy.

IMITATING NATURAL ELEMENTS WITH THREAD

When you create landscape quilts, there are many opportunities for using thread to mimic nature. For example, in *Old World Charm* (page 74), I machine embroidered the trees on the foothills using a sideways, free-motion zigzag stitch. This technique allowed me to create the illusion of trees on top of the foothills. The key to creating trees or foliage on the tops of hills is to use a *matching thread*. The thread blends in with the surrounding area and appears natural.

Trees were embroidered with thread.

To create this stitch, use a matching top thread, set your machine for a wide zigzag stitch, and lower the feed dogs. Use an open-toed machine-embroidery foot. Place your quilt top so that the mountains are facing to the right. You control the width of the stitch, creating the trees on the mountains, by moving the quilt top from side to side.

Use a free-motion zigzag stitch with a matching thread to create trees on top of the foothills.

On the foothills in *Old World Charm*, I created texture with a "fill-in" back-and-forth stitch. This type of fill-in stitch adds texture and the feeling of foliage on the foothills. Make sure your feed dogs are down.

Use a "fill-in" stitch to add dimension to foothills.

THREAD PAINTING

Another option is to create your own machine-embroidered motifs using threads. Thread painting is accomplished using machine-embroidery techniques on a stabilizer in a small embroidery hoop. There are many stabilizers on the market; some dissolve in water, and others disintegrate when touched with a hot iron. Look in quilt shops for stabilizers such as Superior's Dissolve-4X heavy-duty water-soluble stabilizer, Sulky Solvy, Sulky Super Solvy, and Heat Away (see Resources). Try placing two layers of matching tulle between two layers of stabilizer on the top and bottom for additional stability. Trace or copy designs or motifs directly onto the stabilizer and stitch with matching threads to give your quilt an added dimension. Make sure your threads cross each other; otherwise, your motif might fall apart when you remove the stabilizer. Once you have created the motif, remove the stabilizer, let the motif cool or dry, trim the tulle around the edges with sharp embroidery scissors or a stencil cutter, and appliqué the motif to your quilt top with matching threads. This weeping willow tree, below, was created with thread on a stabilizer.

Create a machine-embroidered tree with thread and stabilizer.

Remember, you control the stitch length when you move the fabric. Move up and down or side to side *gradually* to fill in areas. You can use a straight or zigzag stitch with the feed dogs down.

THREAD PLAY ON AN OIL CANVAS

Another good example of how thread can dramatically replicate what is present in nature is reinforced in *Sunshine and Shadows*.

Sunshine and Shadows. Full quilt on page 81.

This landscape quilt is actually another one of my experiments. I enlarged one of my photographs and had it printed on an oil canvas. All of the grain, perspective, and dimensional aspects of this quilt are the direct result of threadwork. Although stitching through the thick oil canvas was somewhat difficult, the machine embroidery really made this quilt dimensional and striking. One of my techniques was to use variegated thread in some of the groupings of flowers. The subtle value changes in the flowers, integrated with small amounts of green foliage, almost make you feel that you are there. The bright chartreuse foliage in the foreground against the dark background makes the foliage pop, whereas the darker green foliage in the background fades away.

Creating realistic clusters of small flowers with a variegated thread is easy once you get the hang of it. The technique is to move the fabric in very small circles next to one another. Once you get a fluid motion going, the thread does the work for you. Come back in with a chartreuse thread to add foliage among the flowers, using the same circular type of stitch.

Create flowers and foliage with tiny circular stitches.

I suggest using a size 75 topstitch or jeans needle when stitching on an oil canvas.

NEEDLE LACE

My description of the machine-embroidery techniques used on *Aloha Spirit* would not be complete unless I included needle lace. Notice the intricate foamy waves hitting the shore. The needle lace for the foamy waves was created by making tiny circles with white thread on a hooped stabilizer. For larger elements, you can create needle lace or thread paint directly onto the quilt top.

Create foamy waves with needle lace.

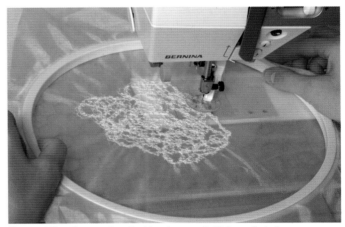

Place stabilizer in a small embroidery hoop and stitch small circles.

Use the same color thread in the bobbin and the needle. *Always* make sure your threads cross when making needle lace; otherwise, you'll end up with a long, stringy mess of thread. After the stabilizer has been removed, let the needle lace dry. Machine appliqué it onto your landscape canvas with a matching thread.

Another great use for needle lace is to create moss for rocks, tree stumps, and so on. Using a bright chartreuse variegated thread and the same circular stitch described earlier, create the moss on a stabilizer, remove the stabilizer, and allow the lace to dry, if necessary. Appliqué the moss onto your quilt. You can also machine embroider the moss directly onto your quilt top, as I did in *Moods of Summer* (full quilt on page 66).

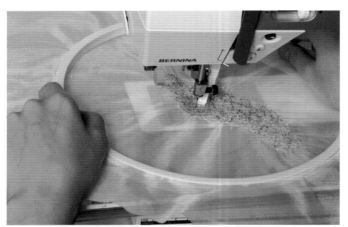

Create realistic "moss" using a circular needle-lace stitch.

CREATING IMAGES WITH RUBBER STAMPS AND THREAD

I find that drawing anything other than a stick figure is a challenge. Creating illusions of landscape elements with thread, however, opens the door to my creativity. I am always searching for ways through the back door, if you will, that allow me to impart a visual element with thread and fabric rather than drawing a realistic impression. Rubber stamping combined with threadwork offers me that opportunity. As described earlier (page 21), I created the boughs of the Douglas fir tree in *Safe Harbor* (full quilt on page 63) by using a rubber stamp on a stabilizer and a thick 30-weight cotton thread. After I stamped the image onto the stabilizer, I hooped and embroidered it. I then removed the stabilizer and appliquéd the shapes onto the quilt top with a matching thread. During the appliqué process, I extended some of the boughs with thread to make them appear feathery and light.

Stamp directly onto a stabilizer using a padded surface, then stitch.

ENHANCING FOLIAGE WITH THREAD

From bushes, grasses, and heavy undergrowth to sparse arid vegetation, foliage seems to appear in most landscape quilts. Enhancing the foliage in your landscape quilts with threadwork creates pizzazz and curiosity. Again, it's the variegated threads that do most of the work for you. Take a look at *Black Beach* (full quilt on page 80) and *Bellows Beach* (full quilt on page 83). The grasses in the lower left corner of *Black Beach* really enhance this quilt.

The foliage in **Black Beach** comes to life with the addition of machine embroidery.

Stitching the grasses and trees isn't difficult. It's basically a back-and-forth stitch. Feel free to insert new grasses with threads, some bending over others, to make them look natural. The same is true for all types of foliage, grass, and tree boughs or needles—you build as you go.

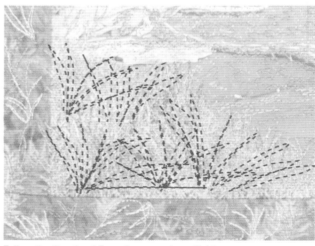

Follow the directional flow of grasses when stitching.

The machine embroidery on the ironwood tree in *Bellows Beach* was accomplished with a thick 30-weight Sulky cotton thread and variegated thread. It really makes the tree look shaggy and wild.

The machine embroidery on the tree in **Bellows Beach** adds realism.

In *Cabin in the Woods* (full quilt on page 76), the pine trees are accented with threads, giving the suggestion of pine needles. Although there is fabric underneath, the thread really adds the feeling of sharp, prickly pine needles. To create this type of sweeping stitch, focus on moving the fabric in the direction you want the pine needles to appear.

Extend the needles on the trees with thread and machine embroidery.

Create a long sweeping stitch. Move the fabric to control where the stitching appears.

Before you begin machine embroidering, look at some photographs of fir trees and their needles for inspiration. Then translate that vision with a matching or variegated thread onto the trees.

I hope this chapter has given you the courage to try machine embroidery in your landscape quilts. Threadwork, to me, is much easier to accomplish than machine quilting. There are no worries about how the quilt top looks on the reverse side, because once the quilt is sandwiched and machine quilted, no one will ever see the back! To reassure you, how about if I bite the bullet and show you the back of one of my quilt tops *after* it has been machine embroidered?

This is the reverse side of a machine-embroidered quilt top.

CHAPTER FIVE

Creating Realistic Elements

This chapter introduces you to techniques that create a variety of natural landscape elements. Although deciding which elements to focus on was difficult, it was you, my readers and students worldwide, who ultimately made the choices. When teaching, I find that some of the most challenging natural elements to duplicate include water, waterfalls, reflections, trees, and mountain ranges. I'll touch on a few fundamentals in each category, in hopes that I will inspire you to take the next step—creating specific realistic elements in your landscape quilts.

Water

Although water might seem easy to create, in practice it is one of the most difficult elements to interpret when creating landscape quilts. Whether it's a calm lake, a tumultuous water-fall, or a stormy sea, water elements need careful thought and execution. In most cases, water needs to be level at the horizon. There are exceptions, though, such as a winding river or a stream moving from the distance to the foreground.

When building a design that includes a water element, such as a lake or an ocean, take the time to measure the horizontal line to be sure it is level and straight. The horizontal straight edge of the water needs to be parallel to the top and bottom edges of the quilt. When you eventually add borders, they must be parallel to the horizontal water line.

Begin with a level horizontal water line.

If you look at *Old World Charm* (full quilt on page 74), for example, you might say, "But Joyce, your horizontal water line isn't level—look at all the little uneven coves along the water's edge!" The coves were added *after* I placed the background water on the canvas, and the water line was horizontally level during the design process.

Reflections

Landscapes that include reflections are popular with my students. Through trial and error, I've worked out some simple techniques for creating reflections. The basic rule of thumb is to remember that to have a reflection, the water needs to be relatively still and quiet. You also need to consider distance and perspective. Let's say you have a mountain scene with trees and a reflecting lake near the bottom edge of the mountain. If the mountains are in the distance and only the trees and foreground are close to the lake, in all probability only the trees and the foreground will reflect in the water. Lynda Sidney's *Pyramid Mountain in Autumn* (full quilt on page 65) is a good example of this scenario.

These are reflections as seen in *Pyramid Mountain in Autumn*.

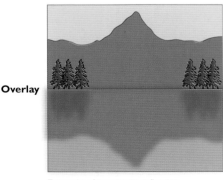

Overlay

If, however, the water is farther from the mountain and the lake is larger in scale, most or all of the mountain will reflect in the water.

Example of mountain reflection

Whether you have a mountain or trees reflecting in water, the method for creating the mirror images is the same. If you are creating a single mountain and its reflection, fold your well-starched fabric (see page 13) in half, wrong sides together, draw the mountain shape, cut it out, and then cut along the fold to separate the mountain from its mirror image.

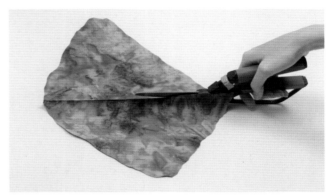

Open the folded mountain and cut along the fold.

To create mirror images of reflecting trees, use the same technique. Fold your well-starched fabric in half, wrong sides together, and cut trees. Open the trees and trim along the fold. It's almost like being back in grade school, cutting out paper dolls!

I used this method in *Reflections* (full quilt on page 61).

Open the tree shapes and cut along the fold.

When you cut out the trees, you will remove a strip of fabric from one edge. Use the leftovers to create rows of trees in the distance on your landscape quilt.

Use the leftovers to create more trees.

Once you've positioned your reflective element(s) on the canvas, add a smooth overlay (see Overlays, page 24) of tulle, netting, or polyester to create the smooth water effect, toning down the value of your reflecting elements.

In *Moods of Summer* (full quilt on page 66), the beautiful fabric creates wonderful mirror-image reflections. The intricate, feathery trees are mirrored in a subtle reflection, making this fabric perfect for creating a dramatic, realistic landscape quilt. An overlay of deep turquoise tulle covers the trees and water, creating the mood of a quiet summer day.

Intricate trees echo with their reflections.

In some cases, it's necessary to include a middle ground when creating reflections. This is basically an area of foreground between the trees or mountains and their reflections, an area where there might be a shoreline. Take another look at *Moods of Summer*. Notice that there is fabric between the trees and their reflections and a layer of moss-green dryer lint collected from felted wool. Half of the dryer lint reflects into the water and is covered with a layer of deep turquoise tulle.

Add a middle ground or shoreline to your landscape.

Waterfalls

Waterfalls are wonderful additions to landscape quilts. Waterfalls add movement, giving the landscape a shift in visual interest. Rough and tumbled, waterfalls are unpredictable and truly add another focal aspect. Creating realistic waterfalls can be challenging, but why not approach it like you are solving a

problem? What fabrics can you *make your own* when designing waterfalls? If a waterfall is the focal point in your landscape quilt, remember to balance it with another natural element. For inspiration, see Chapter 6 for examples of landscape quilts with waterfalls created by my students and peers.

I've designed some waterfall samples to demonstrate several variations on the theme. Using a myriad of fabrics and surface-design techniques and embellishments, you too can make realistic-looking waterfalls.

Cheesecloth Waterfall

This waterfall sample was created using cheesecloth on a fabric mountain background.

Waterfall created with cheesecloth

1. Fold 2 layers of cheesecloth together, placing the raw edges toward the center back.
2. Mold the cheesecloth into a pleasing waterfall shape, keeping the scale consistent with the mountain in the background.
3. Pin the cheesecloth into place.
4. Free-motion stitch the edges with invisible thread.
5. Slice through the *top layer only* of the cheesecloth in 2 or 3 places.
6. Slice through both layers of the cheesecloth in several places.
7. Stitch, using a zigzag stitch with invisible thread, to hold the cheesecloth in place.

Batting and Organza Waterfall

This waterfall sample was created using shredded Hobbs Heirloom batting, white polyester organza, and white Tsukineko ink on a fabric mountain background.

Waterfall created with shredded batting, organza, and ink

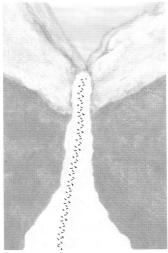
Couch the organza.

1. Cut the batting to the approximate waterfall shape, keeping in mind the scale of the mountains.
2. Shred the batting so there are no blunt or sharp edges.
3. Mold the batting into place and pin it onto your design.
4. Stitch the batting, using a zigzag stitch with invisible thread.
5. Cut slivers of white organza and pin them onto your design.
6. Couch slivers of organza into place with invisible thread, using a zigzag stitch.
7. Add highlights with white Tsukineko ink and a sharp-tipped applicator.

Commercial Fabric and Tulle Waterfall

Fabric, tulle, and painted waterfall

This waterfall sample was created using commercial fabrics, white tulle, Setacolor Opaque Shimmer Pearl textile paint, Jacquard white textile paint, and a medium artist paintbrush on a mountain background.

1. Cut medium blue-and-white fabric into a waterfall shape. Keep in mind the scale of the mountains.

Commercial blue-and-white fabric sample

2. Glue the fabric into place on your canvas.

3. From commercial fabric, cut individual foamy shapes to resemble a bubbling, churning waterfall.
4. Glue the shapes onto your design.
5. Free-motion stitch the shapes with invisible thread.
6. Cut white tulle 2″ larger than the waterfall shape. Fold the edges under to the back.
7. Mold and pin the tulle into place.
8. Free-motion stitch the tulle with invisible thread.
9. Add highlights with textile paints.

Skydyes Fabric and Angelina Fiber Waterfall

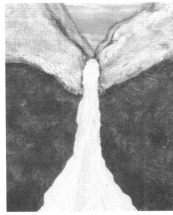
Skydyes fabric and Angelina fiber waterfall

This waterfall sample was created using a hand-painted grayish-blue Mickey Lawler Skydyes fabric (see Resources) and Angelina fiber in Mint Sparkle on a mountain background.

1. Cut a basic waterfall shape from the hand-painted fabric. Keep in mind the scale of the mountains.

2. Glue the shape into place on your canvas.
3. Cut and glue 2 or 3 additional wedge-shaped slivers from the same fabric to make the waterfall seem dimensional.
4. Free-motion stitch the fabrics into place with invisible thread.

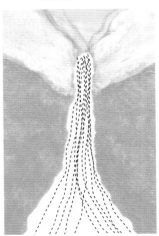
Machine embroider water movements.

5. Machine embroider with a pale blue thread, mimicking water movements in a waterfall.
6. Bond Angelina fiber (see Techniques for Applying Overlays, page 26), mold into place, and pin it over the waterfall. Stitch with invisible thread, using a zigzag stitch.

Remember to press *only from the back* of the quilt top when using Angelina!

Mountains

Creating mountains isn't really difficult once you understand the methodology. In the waterfall samples, I showed you several techniques for creating waterfalls. Now I will lead you through a step-by-step process of creating realistic mountains on your landscape quilts, from mountain background through outcrops. Follow my methodology to make your own mountain-building process easier and to provide new ideas for future landscape quilts.

Background Mountains

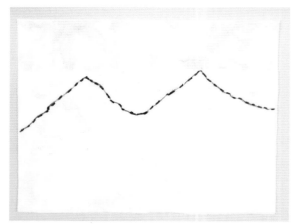

Audition the mountain fabric on your sky background and draw your cutting line directly on the fabric.

This first section addresses auditioning your fabric to get the correct size and position on your canvas. It also describes how to draw your cutting line.

1. Audition the mountain fabric on your sky.

Remember to leave an extra 1″–2″ on the top edge for squaring your quilt. Don't place the mountain fabric too close to the top edge.

2. If you are using a light fabric for the mountain(s), make sure the sky fabric doesn't shadow through. If it does, consider using 2 or more layers of the mountain fabric.

3. Using your visual inspiration as your guide, draw the mountains directly onto the mountain fabric. Start from a middle point and draw outward to the edge; then repeat on the other side. If your first attempt doesn't work, flip the fabric and use the reverse side.

4. Cut just below the drawn line. Position the mountains on the canvas and baste them in place with invisible thread.

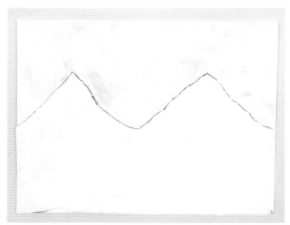

Cut below the drawn line. Highlight the edge with a fabric marker.

5. Highlight the top edge of the mountain with a fabric marker to make it pop against the sky, or consider stitching along the top edge of the mountain with a darker-value thread.

Mountains With Outcroppings and Secondary Mountain Ranges

Cut small rock outcroppings from fabric.

This next section shows how the mountains look when enhanced with fabric for the rock outcroppings.

1. Using a multivalued dark gray-blue fabric, cut small shapes that resemble rock outcroppings.

2. If desired, cut and position light-value fabrics on one side of the mountain and darker values on the other side to imply the direction of the sun and shading.

3. Cut a curvy shape from the same dark gray-blue fabric for the bottom edge of the mountains, creating a secondary mountain range. Baste in place with invisible thread.

Mountains With Dryer Lint and Organza Overlays

Use dryer lint overlays.

This section demonstrates how to incorporate dryer lint and organza as overlays.

1. Place small amounts of dark gray dryer lint on top of the mountains to resemble rock outcroppings.
2. Thin the dryer lint with your fingernails so it isn't too puffy.
3. Place 1 or 2 layers of white polyester organza over the mountain shapes.
4. Extend the organza over the top edge of the mountains.
5. Free-motion stitch the fabrics into place with invisible thread.
6. Trim away excess organza from the top edge.
7. Trim the bottom mountain fabric, if necessary, and glue it into place on top of the organza.

Mountains With Ink and Puff Paint Outcroppings

Use ink and puff paint for outcroppings.

This section demonstrates how to incorporate inks and paints onto your mountains. Your goal is to make the outcroppings look natural. Use photographs for inspiration.

1. Use gray Tsukineko ink and a sharp-tipped applicator to apply rock outcroppings on the mountains.
2. Create dark foothills with dark blue or gray fabric.
3. Apply small amounts of white puff paint on the dark foothills, thinning with a small artist paintbrush if necessary.

Trees

Trees automatically add scale and perspective to our landscapes. Something as simple as a tree can indicate distance and can pull your piece together. Take a look at the Douglas fir tree in the foreground of *Safe Harbor* (full quilt on page 63). The scale of the tree indicates that it's in the foreground, whereas the trees in the background are smaller, thus farther away.

The scale of the foreground tree helps give perspective.

Each tree has its own individual personality, and no two trees are alike. Trees sometimes grow grouped together in stands or groves. Other times you'll see a single tree, such as a stately oak, dominating the scene. When adding trees to your landscape quilts, look to nature for clues. Do the trees pictured in your landscape naturally occur in groupings, or do they stand alone?

The trunks, bark, limbs, twigs, boughs, and needles on trees are also specific for each tree type. When you look at a tree, look at the height. Notice how many limbs break away from the main trunk. Is the trunk gnarled and curvy, or does it grow ramrod straight into the heavens? Are there boughs of leaves or

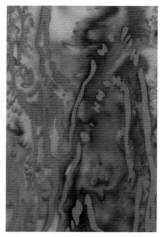

When selecting bark fabric, pay attention to the scale.

individual serrated leaves? Perhaps there are clusters of needles. Which way do the clusters point: up, down, or somewhere in the middle? The questions go on and on. To create successful trees, first study the type of trees you want in your landscape. Shop for fabrics that imitate the look and values of the leaves and bark. Scale is also important when shopping for appropriate fabrics for trees.

Special effects and embellishments can always be added to *make your tree fabric your own.* Think about using fabric markers, inks, or threads to add detail to your trees. On aspen trees, for example, it's easy to add the little black spots and squiggles on the bark with fabric markers, paint, or inks (see *Aspens* by Georgia McRae on page 72).

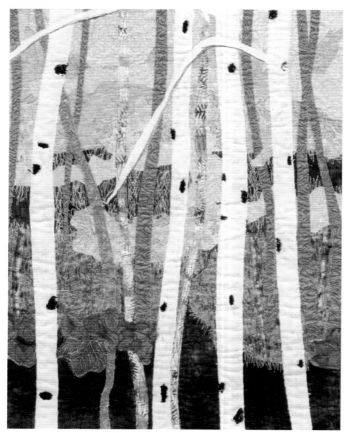

Georgia McRae used fabric markers to add details to her aspen trees.

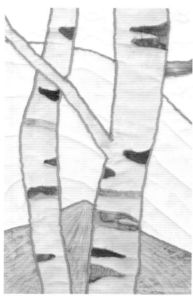

Mona Hutchinson went in a different direction. In *Fairytale Wood* (page 68), Mona used commercial fabrics to add detail to her trees.

Julia Laylander often uses her pinking shears to cut clumps of leaves, giving the edges a serrated, leafy appearance (see *Waterfall,* by Julia Laylander, page 52).

Use fabric to add details to a tree trunk.

Use pinking shears to create a leafy appearance on the tree boughs.

Use machine embroidery to enhance trees.

In *Assiniboine Mist* (page 76), Connie Morrison enhanced the trees by embroidering with threads of different values, making the trees appear natural and shaggy.

Trees are important ingredients in landscape quilts, so I have selected a few of my favorites to demonstrate my techniques.

Douglas Fir Tree

To create a Douglas fir tree:

1. Use a medium-dark green fabric with several values. Starch your fabric.
2. Trace the illustration of the Douglas fir tree onto paper.
3. Enlarge, reduce, or make a mirror-image copy, if desired.
4. Glue the paper pattern with repositionable spray adhesive onto the wrong side of the tree fabric.
5. Cut the tree boughs, using the paper pattern as a guide.
6. Position the tree on the canvas and glue it into place.

Stay away from fabrics that read as solids. Your trees will be more interesting if they include several values. Batiks are especially good for creating trees.

Douglas fir tree created from fabric

Red Maple Tree

To create a red maple tree:

1. Use a multivalued red fall fabric for the tree boughs and use a bark-like medium brown fabric for the tree trunk. Starch the fabrics.

2. Trace the illustration of the red maple tree onto paper.

3. Enlarge, reduce, or make a mirror-image copy of the tree, if desired.

4. Cut out and glue the paper pattern pieces with repositionable spray adhesive onto the wrong side of the fabrics.

5. Cut a tree trunk and several skinny limbs from the brown fabric.

6. Position the tree trunk and limbs onto the canvas and glue them into place.

7. Cut clumps of leaves from the red bough fabric; position and glue them into place on the canvas.

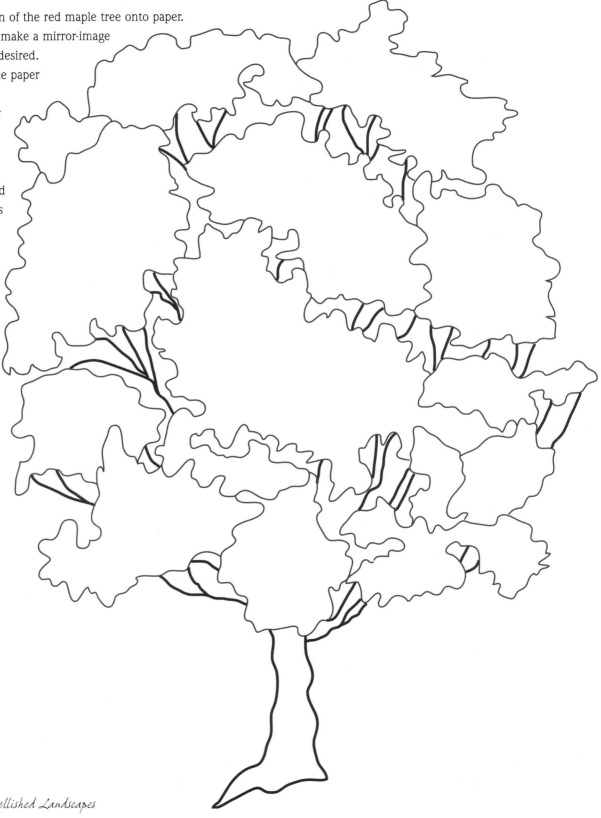

The images below show the individual elements of the tree and how they were cut.

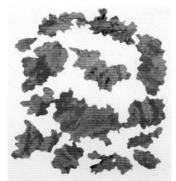

Tree trunk and branches of a red maple tree

Red maple tree foliage

To create a spring or summer version of the tree, substitute the red fall fabric with a medium-value green batik fabric with hints of yellow and chartreuse.

Completed red maple tree in fall colors

Red maple tree in spring or summer

Rustic Pine Tree

Using the methods described for the red maple tree (page 44), create a fabric rustic pine tree. Use a medium-value green fabric to create the tree and tree trunk.

Completed fabric rustic pine tree

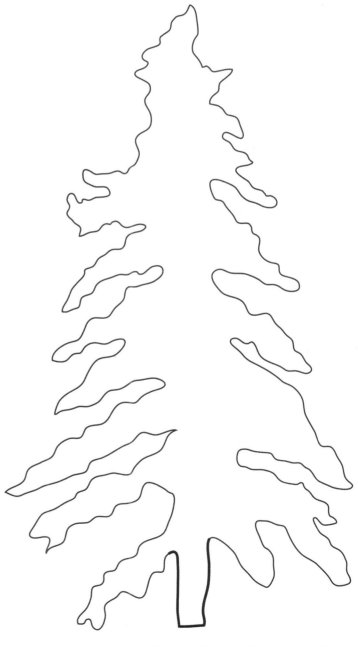

Palm Tree

Using the methods described for the red maple tree (page 44), create a fabric palm tree. Use a multi-valued medium green-and-gold fabric for the palm fronds and a light to medium gray-brown fabric for the tree trunk.

Completed fabric palm tree

Flowering Dogwood Tree

Using the methods described for the red maple tree (page 44), create a fabric flowering dogwood tree. Use a medium- to light-value pink fabric for the flowers and a light-value brown fabric for the tree bark. Use a brown fabric marker to add small branches. If desired, sponge over the pink flowers with white textile paint or ink.

Completed fabric flowering dogwood tree

Sugar Pine Tree

Using the methods described for the red maple tree (page 44), create a fabric sugar pine tree. Use a medium-dark green batik for the tree boughs and a medium brown bark-like fabric for the tree trunk.

Completed fabric sugar pine tree

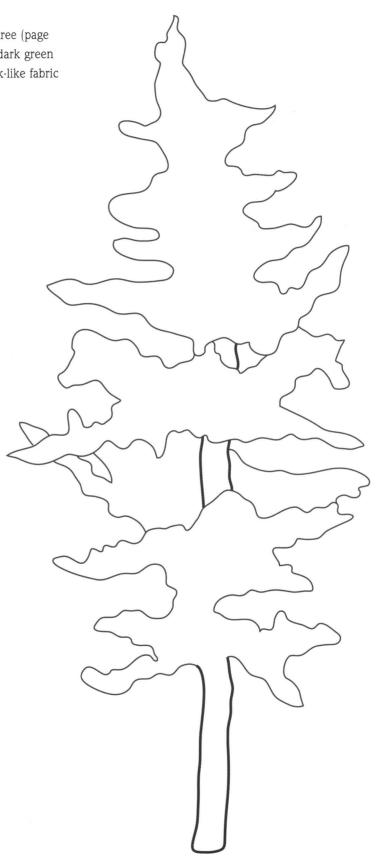

Oak Tree

Using the methods described for the red maple tree (page 44), create a fabric oak tree. Use a multivalued green fabric with lights, mediums, and darks for the tree boughs and a medium brown, gnarly, bark-like fabric for the tree trunk and limbs. Cut tree boughs, making the edges appear filigreed, like small leaves.

Completed fabric oak tree

I hope this chapter has given you insight into creating natural elements and has encouraged you to try new methods to create your own unique interpretations.

Projects & Inspiration

CHAPTER SIX

Photograph by Valori Wells

Whispering Waterfalls

Now that I've given you the tips, techniques, and tools to create beautifully embellished landscapes, it's time to introduce you to the quilts and their makers, along with projects created just for you! Waterfalls seem to be a particularly intriguing subject, so we'll start our journey there.

Waterfall

Inspiration and Basics

Julia Laylander's quilts are often cobbled together from many different memories of places and times in her life. Calling herself a "visually oriented" person, Julia finds creating art quilts an "immensely satisfying pastime." Although Julia is self-taught, she says books, including *Luscious Landscapes,* have helped her along her way. An extremely chemically sensitive person, Julia uses only non-toxic and odor-free materials when creating her art quilts. For example, she uses glue sticks rather than spray glues, as well as odorless water-based inks and paints (see Resources for more about Julia's quilts).

When using a glue stick, Julia recommends carefully applying glue near the edges of the fabric pieces. She is able to skip the basting process using this method because the glue holds the fabric pieces in place until she is ready to machine quilt.

Making the Fabric Her Own

To add shimmer to the pond, Julia experimented with Perfect Pearls embossing powder (see Resources) mixed with a tiny bit of water and painted directly onto the fabric with a small paintbrush. Julia also uses pinking shears to cut most of her bushes, trees, grasses, and other foliage. She often cuts them out using a sort of "Swiss cheese"

Waterfall, Julia A. Laylander, Yachats, Oregon, 16″ × 20″, 2003.

approach—cutting holes in the fabric and going around the edges with pinking shears. Instead of having lots of little pieces for a tree, for example, she sometimes uses one piece of fabric that is "holey."

Amy's Time Out, Kay Sheridan, Missoula, Montana, 29″ × 27″, 2005.

Amy's Time Out

Inspiration and Basics

An avid horseback rider, Kay Sheridan frequently rides "up the Snake" to visit this peaceful vista in the Rattlesnake Wilderness in Lolo National Forest, Montana. Her mountain valley scene, complete with indigenous ponderosa pine trees, a whispering waterfall, ferns, moss, and a deer standing in the shadows, captures the serene mood and makes you feel like you are a part of the setting. Kay says, "I find inspiration around every corner. People, places, colors, and patterns all set my creative juices flowing." Kay spent hours playing with fabrics to create exactly the right mood. She incorporated overlays of tulle to get shadows in the forest and in the water; she also added sparkly netting over the falls and pond to mimic the sun dancing on the water. Kay fashioned needle lace to make the ferns and the moss.

Making the Fabric Her Own

This poignant and heartwarming quilt includes Kay's "very special daughter-in-law," Amy. Sitting under a giant ponderosa pine tree, Amy hugs her dog Wriggley. Kay used a photograph of Amy and her dog to help get the correct scale and values.

The Waterfall

Inspiration and Basics

I challenged my friend Sonia Grasvik, one of the most talented fiber artists on the planet, to create a waterfall scene for this book. I knew whatever she created would be spectacular, and, as always, she exceeded my wildest expectations. Inspired by a painting, *Fuji From the Mountains of ISU, #22,* by Ando or Utagawa Hiroshige (1797–1858), Sonia's striking interpretation literally takes my breath away. Sonia shows no fear when treading into unknown territories. She made the mountains, the clouds, and the waterfall separately on polyester organza bonded onto Sulky Totally Stable iron-on stabilizer and appliquéd them to the quilt. This quilt was initially "all about the waterfall," but as it progressed, it ultimately ended up being "all about the trees," which were individually machine embroidered entirely with thread.

Making the Fabric Her Own

To create the stunning waterfall, Sonia "captured" Angelina fibers under blue nylon tulle layered on top of commercial fabric, and she embellished the waterfall with sparkling threads. Sonia's creative border treatment includes Seminole piecing and Asian coins.

The Waterfall, Sonia Grasvik, Seattle, Washington, 32″ × 37″, 2005. Photograph courtesy of Ken Wagner.

Lake Garibaldi Revisited, Lynne Goulette, Grants Pass, Oregon, 33″ × 31″, 2004.

Inspiration and Basics

Lynne Goulette, who has a background in design and color, says, "Integrating traditional and innovative quilting techniques into fabric is a means of expressing my inner voice and life experiences."

Lynne's electrifying quilt *Lake Garibaldi Revisited* resulted from a photograph she took while hiking with family in Garibaldi Provincial Park in British Columbia. After a grueling five-mile hike, "we crossed a bridge, and there was this most gorgeous turquoise glacial lake," says Lynne. She snapped an inspirational photograph as they crossed the bridge at the outflow of the lake. You can easily see why Lynne's quilts have been featured and have won ribbons at local events and museums near her home in Grants Pass, Oregon.

Lynne used my basic landscape techniques to create her quilt and also projected her photograph onto a large piece of paper, tracing some of the elements to use as templates.

Making the Fabric Her Own

As you can see from the photograph of the quilt, Lynne created a stunning, one-of-a-kind waterfall. She admits that she stepped out of her comfort zone: "It was fun to get brave with the waterfall, adding the variety of threads, wool, and embellishments."

Lynne stabilized a light blue batik fabric, instead of muslin, for her canvas, eliminating the need to add a sky background layer. She also used fusible web to add elements to her canvas; as a result she did not need to prestarch her fabrics.

Materials

- Sky/water canvas, light blue batik (instead of muslin) for canvas: 1 yard, trimmed to 33″ × 31″
- Distant mountains, 3 values of blue-gray batik: 1 yard total
- Trees, medium-dark green batik: ¹/₂ yard

- Tree trunks and wood in stream, bark-like brown fabric: $1/2$ yard
- Foreground mountains, multicolored brown, gold, blue, and green fabric: $1/2$ yard
- Rocks, variety of values of green and gold batiks: 4 fat quarters
- Water overlay, white tulle: $1/2$ yard
- Inner border, rust batik: $3/8$ yard
- Outer border (top and sides) and bottom border, medium-dark green batik: $3/4$ yard
- Binding, dark green batik: $3/8$ yard
- Backing and sleeve: $1\frac{3}{8}$ yards
- Batting: $37'' \times 35''$
- Lightweight fusible interfacing for canvas and borders
- Spray starch
- Steam-A-Seam 2 fusible web: $3/4$ yard
- Threads: invisible, variety of matching silk (including green) and variegated cotton, and silver metallic embroidery
- Rough-spun natural wool, white and off-white: various lengths for couching on waterfall
- Silk ribbon, light pink for couching on waterfall
- Fabric markers for shading on rocks (optional): green, gray, and brown

Cutting

Inner border, mitered: Cut 4 strips $1\frac{1}{4}'' \times$ width of fabric.

Outer border, top and sides, mitered: Cut 3 strips $4\frac{1}{2}'' \times$ width of fabric.

Bottom border: Cut 1 strip $4\frac{1}{2}''$ wide on each end and widening to $7\frac{1}{2}''$ for the curved center $\times$ width of fabric (see quilt photograph).

Binding: Cut 4 strips $2\frac{1}{2}'' \times$ width of fabric.

Sleeve: Cut 1 strip $8\frac{1}{2}'' \times$ width of fabric.

Construction

Refer to Chapters 1, 2, and 5.

1. Press all the wrinkles out of the background sky/water fabric. Stabilize the sky/water fabrics with lightweight fusible interfacing.
2. Starch the mountain, water, tree, tree trunk, driftwood, and rock fabrics.
3. Cut, position, and glue the mountains and water into place. *Optional:* Make a full-scale drawing of your design, then cut out small pieces to use as paper templates.
4. Follow the manufacturer's directions to apply fusible web to the *wrong* side of the fabrics for small pieces, such as trees, tree trunks, driftwood, and rocks.
5. Cut out the small elements and arrange them on the canvas. Tuck the trees behind the mountains in the foreground. Fuse in place.
6. Position overlays of tulle, wool, and batting over the water and pin them into place.
7. Cut, audition, position, and glue the rocks and driftwood in the water.
8. Baste the entire composition with invisible thread. Trim excess tulle, wool, and batting, as necessary.

Special Effects and Finishing

Refer to Chapters 3, 4, and 12.

1. Enhance the landscape with free-motion machine embroidery.
   - Embroider over trees, rocks, and mountains with matching variegated cotton threads.
   - Use silk thread to add free-motion swirls to the water for movement.
   - Mimic moss on rocks with tight free-motion swirls and green silk thread.
2. If desired, add shading to the rocks with fabric markers. Heat set, as necessary.
3. Steam the canvas from the back. Square the canvas and add stabilized borders.

The bottom border needs to be cut separately and curved down, following the natural flow of the waterfall.

4. Cut, position, and glue pieces of wool, silk ribbon, and silver metallic threads over the bottom border, emulating a waterfall flowing over the edge of the border. Couch embellishments into place with invisible thread and a zigzag stitch.
5. Sandwich your quilt. Add a label. Quilt, block, and square the quilt. Add binding and a sleeve, and you're done!

The Easy Version

Don't carry the waterfall over the edge of the borders. Cut the bottom border the same size as the other 3 outer borders. Cut all shapes freehand instead of tracing, and use glue instead of fusible web.

CHAPTER SEVEN

Photograph by Valori Wells

Stately Structures

In this chapter, we explore a variety of quilts: from a twelfth-century castle packed with history, to quaint country cottages, to an old weathered barn. Memorable places often trigger poignant memories of times past and are perfect inspirations for landscape quilts.

Pernstejn

Inspiration and Basics

Captivated and enchanted by a visit to the Pernstejn Castle in the Czech Republic, Peggy Holt captured memories by taking snapshots during her visit. Bubbling with enthusiasm, Peggy says, "I could almost see the ladies in their flowing gowns sweeping down the hallways; the knights as they returned from a skirmish, their swords clanking against their armor; and the horses' hooves clip-clopping along on the cobblestones. My quilt pays homage to the castle, which was built in the twelfth century—it truly is a mystical and magical place." *Pernstejn* was featured at the International Quilt Festival in Houston, Texas, in the fall of 2004.

Armed with a variety of fabrics perfect for a castle scene, Peggy joined a workshop I taught in Missoula, Montana. Peggy says, "I loved every stage when creating this quilt because it was new to me. I enjoyed the quest of finding the right combinations of value, color, and scale in fabrics."

Making the Fabric Her Own

Without hesitation, Peggy cut into her fabrics, creating perfect angles to form her castle. I was totally amazed at her uncanny ability to add shadows and dimension with watercolor crayons and pencils during the workshop. Instead of accomplishing machine embroidery and quilting on a standard machine, Peggy opted to quilt and embellish her landscape quilt on her Gammill longarm machine.

Pernstejn, Peggy Holt, Missoula, Montana, 31″× 44″, 2004.

Quiet Time

Quiet Time, Linda Cotant, Missoula, Montana, 30″ × 37″, 2004.

Inspiration and Basics

Linda Cotant was inspired by her love of a quiet, old-fashioned cottage garden, "just like Grandma had." Working from memory, Linda created this delightful quilt in one of my workshops. She once remarked, "You'll never see me quilting—that's for old ladies." But now she admits, "Either I've gotten old, or I just got the bug!" A quilter of only five years, Linda loves working with color and finds the results rewarding.

Making the Fabric Her Own

Rather than incorporating overlays or using paint, Linda says her favorite part was working with the fence and the roses in the foreground of the quilt. When she added those elements, they seemed to make the quilt pop. Linda's unique treatment with the roses falling over the borders is charming, as is the extensive machine embroidery with a variety of threads.

Skye Cottage, Hawkshead, Cumbria

Inspiration and Basics

Using a photograph for inspiration, Carol Robinson recreated the quaint cottage she and her family rented while on a family vacation in the Lake District of England, using fabric as her medium. Carol was a student in a workshop I taught in Plaistow, New Hampshire, and her design quickly took shape on the wall. She says, "Learning to break the rules of traditional quilting was my greatest accomplishment in this quilt, and incorporating Joyce's techniques allowed me the freedom of design." She had the "bones" of this quilt completed by the end of our one-day workshop, and that she added very little to the design after she got home. Once her quilt design is complete, Carol likes to pin it onto her design wall and "live with it" for a while.

Making the Fabric Her Own

Intrigued with her new sewing machine, Carol experimented with some of the decorative stitches from the machine's menu, incorporating them into her design. Many of the flowers were stitched with decorative threads using the menu stitches.

Skye Cottage, Hawkshead, Cumbria, Carol Robinson, Rye, New Hampshire, 28″ × 26″, 2004.

Inspiration and Basics

After teaching at a symposium in New Zealand in 2001, my husband and I stayed with symposium organizers Dorothy and Barrie Smith on their dairy farm. While taking us on a tour of the farm, Barrie decided to move some of the cows from one paddock to another. To attract their attention, he shouted, "Come on. Come on." I'll be darned if the cows didn't come *running* up to him. It was one of the funniest sights I've ever seen. This quilt was inspired by that visit and by a request from my son and daughter-in-law for an original landscape quilt for Christmas. This quilt was fun and fast. Once the background fabrics were on the canvas, the other elements just fell into place.

Caleb, Waiting for the Cows to Come Home, Joyce R. Becker, Kent, Washington, from the collection of the Shawn Becker family, 27″ × 30″, 2004.

Making the Fabric My Own

Sometimes, it's fun just to let your imagination fly. In this quilt, I dabbled with Tsukineko inks to manipulate the barn and the roof fabrics, sponged a myriad of ink colors on the tree bark, and enhanced the fence with a fabric marker. I did a Google search on the Internet and found copyright-free photographs of Holstein cows and enlarged and printed them on pretreated computer fabric. I took a digital photograph of my grandson Caleb and printed the image on pretreated computer fabric. I used a VersaCraft stamp pad to rubber stamp the meadow grasses onto the pasture.

Materials

- Stabilized muslin canvas: 27″ × 30″
- Sky, bright blue fabric with scattered white clouds: $\frac{1}{2}$ yard
- Pasture, bright green chartreuse fabric: 1 yard
- Mountains, medium to dark gray fabric with snow-capped glaciers: $\frac{1}{2}$ yard
- Trees and leaves, multivalued fabric, from light to dark green: $\frac{1}{2}$ yard
- Barn, medium red plank-like fabric: $\frac{1}{4}$ yard
- Barn roof, roof-like dark gray to light black fabric: $\frac{1}{4}$ yard
- Tree trunk, limbs, and twigs, medium-dark brown bark-like fabric: $\frac{1}{4}$ yard
- Fence and fence posts, medium to light brown fabric with wood grain: $\frac{1}{2}$ yard
- Inner border, dark red mottled fabric: $\frac{1}{4}$ yard
- Outer border and binding, multivalued green mottled or batik fabric: $\frac{7}{8}$ yard

- Backing and sleeve: 1¼ yards
- Batting: 31″ × 34″
- Lightweight fusible interfacing for canvas and borders
- Spray starch
- Freezer paper
- Tsukineko All-Purpose Ink: white, chocolate, and gray
- Fantastix applicators: sharp-tipped and bullet-tipped
- Tsukineko VersaCraft stamp pad, pine green
- Rubber stamp: meadow grasses
- Fabric markers: chocolate and yellow
- Threads: invisible, matching, and variegated, 30-weight cotton, to match cows and flowers
- Pretreated computer fabric for inkjet printing

Cutting

Inner border, mitered: Cut 4 strips 1″ × width of fabric.
Outer border, mitered: Cut 4 strips 4″ × width of fabric.
Binding: Cut 4 strips 2½″ × width of fabric.
Sleeve: Cut 1 strip 8½″ × width of fabric.

Construction

Refer to Chapters 1 and 2.

1. Follow the instructions for creating a canvas.
2. Audition your fabrics on your design wall.
3. Press the sky and pasture background fabrics and glue them into place.
4. Starch all the other fabrics.
5. Audition, cut, and glue the mountains into place.
6. Audition, cut, and glue the trees in the distance onto the canvas. To give the appearance of distance, consider using the wrong (lighter) side of the fabric.
7. Refer to the photograph of the quilt as a guide to draw a barn onto the dull side of freezer paper. Audition the barn on your canvas, making size adjustments if necessary. Cut the freezer paper apart so you have templates for the barn and the barn roof.
8. Iron the freezer paper templates, shiny side down, onto the front side of the barn fabrics; cut. Remove the freezer paper and glue the barn onto your canvas.
9. Audition bark-like fabric for the tree. Cut, position, and glue the tree in place.
10. Cut clumps of leaves from the starched, multivalued green leaf fabric. Position and glue the leaves into place.
11. Print the cows on the pretreated computer fabric. Let dry, then cut out the cows. Position and glue them into place.
12. Audition fence fabric. Cut, position, and glue the fence in place.
13. Baste the entire composition with invisible thread.

Special Effects and Finishing

Refer to Chapters 3, 4, and 12.

1. Place your canvas on a protected wall surface before you begin painting with inks. Add details to the landscape with all-purpose inks and markers.
   - Paint tree bark and limbs.
   - Form planks on the barn and add detail to the roof.
   - Add definition to the fence and fence posts with a chocolate-colored fabric marker.
   - Enhance a few of the meadow grass flowers with a yellow marker.
2. Rubber stamp meadow grasses onto the pasture, starting in the background and working forward.
3. Enhance the landscape with free-motion machine embroidery.
   - Use dark gray thread to add detail to the planks and roof of the barn.
   - Use a figure-eight stitch and variegated green thread to embroider clumps of leaves on the tree.
   - Simulate bark on the tree trunk, using a variegated brown thread and elongated stitches.
   - Embroider cows with black and white threads.
   - Outline the fence with variegated brown thread.
   - Add detail to the meadow grasses with a variegated green thread.
   - Accent a few of the meadow grass flowers with a matching yellow thread.
4. Steam the canvas from the back. Square the canvas and add stabilized borders.
   Optional: Position an image (like the one I used of Caleb) into place over the stabilized borders. Baste the image in place with invisible thread.
5. Sandwich your quilt. Add a label. Quilt, block, and square the quilt. Add binding and a sleeve, and you're done!

The Easy Version

Shop for barnyard animals already printed on commercial fabrics, such as pigs, horses, chickens, or cows. Replace the cows with the preprinted animals. Skip the rubber stamping.

CHAPTER EIGHT

Water, Water Everywhere

Why is water so cathartic, mesmerizing, and hypnotic? For me, the sound and sight of water evoke calmness and peace. The gentle trickle of a stream or tumultuous waves breaking and crashing onto the beach can be the impetus for stunning landscape quilts. In this chapter, we discover how to create water-inspired quilts, including sheltered bays, reflecting lakes, a peaceful pond, and a tropical paradise complete with a beautiful beach.

Photograph by Valori Wells

Night Fisherman

Inspiration and Basics

Rosellen Carolan fondly remembers "Henry the Heron," who occasionally perched on a buoy outside her bedroom each day. Rosy is a multitalented quilt artist, and her quilts have won numerous awards, including a ribbon at the prestigious International Quilt Festival in Houston, Texas. Her work has also appeared in several quilting books. An ongoing project for many years, *Night Fisherman* finally came together when Rosy discovered the "perfect" water fabric. By that time, she says, "I found that I had developed many more skills and felt I could finish the piece successfully." Rosy went as far as cutting a fresh cattail, which she kept in her studio to refer to while working on the quilt. She used wool to give texture to the cattails in the quilt, and she used a variety of values for the leaves, placing the lightest in the distance. The heron was built in separate units and machine appliquéd onto the quilt with a zigzag stitch.

Making the Fabric Her Own

Rosy said her goal with this piece was to get the "feel of the large bird in its surroundings." She left the paper heron pattern pinned to the background to help with the placement of the other elements during the design process. Rosy says, "I enjoy the freedom of using free-cut, raw-edged fabric, moving and repositioning

Night Fisherman, Rosellen Carolan, Auburn, Washington, 56″ × 65″, 2004.

pieces as I build the picture." The wispy needle-lace feathers on the heron were created with thread using water-soluble Solvy and netting in an embroidery hoop.

Reflections, Joyce R. Becker, Kent, Washington, 25″ × 25″, 2005.

Reflections

Inspiration and Basics

I designed and created *Reflections* because I wanted to include at least one quilt with reflections in this book. My goal was to create a soft, pastel sky that reflected into the water. Artfabrik by Laura Wasilowski (see Resources), a beautiful hand-dyed fabric, was perfect for the sky and the reflection. Using this fabric for my canvas, I added rows of foothills in the background and an island. The trees and their subtle reflections in the water created just the mood I sought.

The lush foliage in the foreground was added after the stabilized borders were attached to the quilt. I used two layers of a "leafy" commercial fabric bonded together and basted them to the quilt with invisible thread. The groupings of leaves and flowers were embellished with machine embroidery.

Making the Fabric My Own

I incorporated several innovative techniques into this quilt for visual impact. For example, I rubber stamped the tree boughs on the upper right onto the background fabric with a green ink and enhanced them with machine embroidery. I drew the branches and twigs with a brown fabric marker. The glowing sun on the horizon was created with a subtle yellow fabric and an overlay of yellow bondable Angelina fiber. To add reflections of the sky in the water, I painted the water with soft pink and yellow textile paints. Overlays of white tulle and organza were added on the quilt top, followed by a thin layer of purple Angelina in the water and an overlay of mauve tulle.

Aloha Spirit, Joyce R. Becker, Kent, Washington, 42″ × 44″, 2004.

Aloha Spirit

Inspiration and Basics

Ever since my husband retired, we've taken an annual vacation to Hawaii. While there, I've taught and lectured on most of the islands. This quilt pays homage to the lush, green tropical paradise; mesmerizing ocean and easy-going, friendly locals who make the trip worthwhile. The fragrant flowers coupled with the warm, soft breezes and the repetitious sound of the waves crashing on the shore beckon me even now! Shopping for the fabrics for this quilt was pure delight. I discovered the perfect hand-painted green for the mountains and the blue for the sky fabric on Mickey Lawler's Skydyes website (see Resources). While teaching in Maui, I found a vintage Hawaiian fabric with palm trees in just the right scale.

Making the Fabric My Own

Special effects and embellishments were crucial to this design. I incorporated several overlays, textile paints, inks, and fabric markers. After the design was complete, I placed an overlay of turquoise netting over the water to emulate movement. A second overlay of sapphire blue tulle in the deeper water creates depth and perspective. The breaking waves were painted with opaque and pearlized textile paints. A layer of rosy taupe organza was appliquéd over the sand fabric at the edge of the water to give the appearance of wet sand. I created the white needle lace on water-soluble stabilizer and appliquéd it onto the shoreline to create the foamy waves. The palm tree fronds were enhanced with inks, fabric markers, and thick cotton embroidery thread; the horizontal lines on the bark were painted with white ink.

Safe Harbor

Inspiration and Basics

As a faculty member for the 2003 Gig Harbor Quilt Festival, in Gig Harbor, Washington, I was asked to donate a wallhanging for an auction that would benefit the Breast Cancer Awareness Foundation. The theme was "harbor reflections." Using a compilation of photographs and postcards from the Gig Harbor area, I designed a picturesque scene with Mount Rainier in the distance; trees in the middle ground and water, sailboats, and a giant Douglas fir tree in the foreground. My challenge was to create a calming scene that would raise some money for this worthy organization.

This project is a basic design easy enough for beginning landscape quilters. With good background fabrics, the quilt comes together quickly.

Making the Fabric My Own

Creating rocky outcroppings on white mountains with colored dryer lint is so much fun!

Lint collected after you dry a load of blue jeans is the perfect color and value for these overlays. Consider using more than one value of lint, shading half of the outcroppings with a lighter value and the other side with a darker value to indicate the direction of the sun. Use very small bits of lint instead of big clumps, and thin it out in all directions with your fingernails or a bamboo skewer.

Safe Harbor, Joyce R. Becker, Kent, Washington, 30˝ × 15˝, 2003, from the collection of Lisa Gately. Photograph courtesy of Ken Wagner.

Materials

- Stabilized muslin canvas: 30˝ × 15˝
- Sky, light blue fabric with scattered clouds: $3/4$ yard
- Water, medium blue fabric: $3/4$ yard
- Mountain, solid or mottled white fabric: $1/4$ yard
- Dryer lint: blue
- White organza overlay: $1/4$ yard
- White tulle overlay: $1/4$ yard
- Foothills, medium blue-gray fabric: $1/4$ yard
- Preprinted green tree fabric: $1/2$ yard
- Shoreline, beige fabric: $1/4$ yard
- Sailboat fabric: $1/4$ yard
- Tree trunk, medium-dark brown bark-like fabric: $1/4$ yard
- Foliage, medium to dark green fabric: $1/4$ yard
- Inner border, mottled fuchsia fabric: $1/4$ yard
- Outer border and binding, multivalued mottled green fabric: $3/4$ yard
- Backing and sleeve: $7/8$ yard
- Batting: 34˝ × 19˝
- Lightweight fusible interfacing for canvas and borders
- Spray starch
- Water-soluble stabilizer placed into an embroidery hoop
- Rubber stamp, bough of a Douglas fir tree
- Stamp pad, pine green
- Threads: invisible and green 30-weight cotton to match Douglas fir tree
- Dryer lint from blue jeans
- Small amount of shredded white batting

Thin the bits of dryer lint with your fingernail or a skewer.

Cutting

Inner border, mitered: Cut 3 strips 1¹/₂″ × width of fabric.
Outer border, mitered: Cut 4 strips 3¹/₂″ × width of fabric.
Binding: Cut 3 strips 2¹/₂″ × width of fabric.
Sleeve: Cut 1 strip 8¹/₂″ × width of fabric.

Construction

1. Refer to Chapters 1, 2, 4, and 5. Follow the instructions for creating a canvas.
2. Audition, cut, and glue the sky and water background fabrics to the canvas.
3. Starch all the other fabrics.
4. Sketch the mountain onto white fabric (remember to use several layers if the background shows through the fabric). Cut and glue the mountain to the canvas and baste with invisible thread. To add contrast between the mountain and sky line, highlight the top edge of the mountain with a fabric marker, or stitch along the edge with darker-value thread.
5. Using the photograph as your inspiration, place small bits of dryer lint (resembling rocky outcroppings) onto the mountain; thin with your fingernails.
6. Pin an overlay of white organza over the top of the mountain, extending the overlay into the sky.
7. Audition, cut, and glue the foothills into place. Cover with white tulle.
8. Audition and cut the trees in the distance from the preprinted tree fabric; form uneven tree tops as you cut. Glue the trees into place.
9. Audition, cut, and glue the shoreline fabric.
10. Take the shredded batting and mold it along the shoreline.
11. Cut and glue sailboats onto the water.
12. Baste the entire composition with invisible thread. Trim excess organza and tulle, as necessary.
13. Steam the canvas from the back. Square the canvas and add stabilized borders.

Special Effects and Finishing

Refer to Chapters 3, 4, 5, and 12.

1. Audition, cut, and glue the tree trunk into place, extending it into the stabilized border.
2. Audition, cut, and glue the foliage around the tree trunk. Baste the tree and foliage.
3. Create and appliqué tree boughs to the tree trunk. (See Creating Images With Rubber Stamps and Thread on page 21.)
4. Enhance the landscape with free-motion machine embroidery.

- Using a small circular stitch and a matching thread, embroider over the dryer lint overlays to enhance the outcrop effect.
- With free-form stitches and matching thread, extend some of the tree tops in the distance to create uneven heights.
- Enhance the frothy shoreline by stitching over the shredded batting, hitting the shore with a white thread.
- Augment the water effects with a matching blue thread and elongated horizontal stitches.
- Embroider the Douglas fir tree extensively, adding long wispy pine needles with the matching 30-weight green cotton thread.

Add embroidered foliage around the tree trunk.

5. Sandwich your quilt. Add a label. Quilt, block, and square the quilt. Add binding and a sleeve, and you're done!

The Easy Version

Select and purchase a commercial fabric for the mountain. Purchase a commercial fabric with the right scale trees instead of creating your own. Eliminate the sailboats in the water.

Zack at Great Pond

Inspiration and Basics

Using a photograph of her son Zack when he was just one and a half years old, Cyndy Rymer's quilt captures a special moment from a family vacation. Cyndy loves combining realism and impressionism in landscape quilts and translating photographs into quilts. Cyndy is quite familiar with my techniques, and she combined them with skills developed during a workshop with well-known artist Joan Colvin. Cyndy layered the backing and batting on her design wall and then pinned strips to it until she was happy with the design.

Making the Fabric Her Own

Cyndy incorporated many special effects and embellishing techniques into this quilt, making her design sing with realism. She used textile paints, yarns, overlays of organza, and machine embroidery to create this delightful quilt, printing the photograph of Zack on her Hewlett-Packard all-in-one printer on pretreated computer fabric. Cyndy says, "I love the spontaneity of starting with a blank canvas and adding layers!"

Zack at Great Pond, Cyndy Rymer, Danville, California, 46″× 31″, 2005.

Pyramid Mountain in Autumn

Inspiration and Basics

Lynda Sidney says that after taking my workshop, she is confident and excited about her ability to translate her own photographs and visions into landscape quilts. Inspired by photographs of the Canadian Rockies by Bela Baliko, Lynda said her greatest accomplishment when creating this quilt was giving herself "permission to cut freehand, play with fabrics, make changes, and trust my instincts!" After taking this class, Lynda said, "I now see the landscape possibilities in fabrics that I wouldn't have previously considered." An award-winning traditional quilter, Lynda plans to create more landscape quilts in the future.

Making the Fabric Her Own

When I saw the fabric Lynda had selected for the mountains in the distance, I was a bit hesitant. As her design grew, however, I knew Lynda had made the right choice. The moral of this story? Trust your gut instinct! Lynda manipulated the remainder of the fabric she used in the foreground until she captured just the right value for the reflection.

Pyramid Mountain in Autumn, Lynda Sidney, Canmore, Alberta, 36″× 32″, 2005, inspired by a photograph by Bela Baliko.

Moods of Summer, Joyce R. Becker, Kent, Washington, 44″ × 43″, 2005.

Inspiration and Basics

There are times in life when fabrics speak to you. You haven't a clue what you will do with the fabric, but you *just know* you have to have it. When I teach at the International Quilt Festival in Houston, Texas, my first vendor stop is Mickey Lawler's Skydyes booth, where I drop most of my earnings. During my last visit, a yellow-and-purple streaked fabric called my name. I put it down and picked it up several times. I took that as a sign from above and bought it. The same thing happened when I saw the McKenna Ryan Hoffman fabric I used in this quilt. Somewhere, in the dark depths of my consciousness, my mind was putting these two fabrics together, telling me they would work cohesively. With just two delightful and highly compatible fabrics, this landscape quilt seemed to design itself. The beauty of the quilt is the simplicity of the design. Cluttering it up with more "stuff" seemed superfluous.

Making the Fabric My Own

I added mossy-looking dryer lint under the rocks with lint collected by a friend from felted green wool. I machine embroidered additional moss with a matching thread. To make the reflection more natural, I used an overlay of deep turquoise over the reflection of the trees and moss.

Materials

- Hand-painted yellow-and-purple streaked Mickey Lawler Skydyes (instead of muslin) fabric for canvas: 1¼ yards, trimmed to 44″ × 43″
- Mountains in foreground, rose and purple batiks: ½ yard
- Mountains in distance, green, turquoise, and purple batiks: ½ yard
- Sky and water, purple and yellow fabrics: 1 yard total
- Trees, preprinted fabric: ½ yard

- Boulders, a variety of brown, gray, and purple fabrics: $1/4$-yard cuts
- Shoreline, medium purple fabric: $1/4$ yard
- Dark turquoise bridal illusion tulle: $3/4$ yard
- Inner border, subtle moss green–and–beige stripe fabric: $3/8$ yard
- Outer border and binding, rosy batik with hints of purple: $1 1/8$ yards
- Backing and sleeve: 3 yards
- Batting: $48" \times 47"$
- Lightweight fusible interfacing for canvas and borders
- Spray starch
- Threads: invisible and matching
- Dryer lint, green

Cutting

Inner border, mitered: Cut 5 strips $2" \times$ width of fabric.
Outer border, mitered: Cut 5 strips $4" \times$ width of fabric.
Binding: Cut 5 strips $2 1/2" \times$ width of fabric.
Sleeve: Cut 1 strip $8 1/2" \times$ width of fabric.

Construction

Refer to Chapters 1, 2, 4, 5, and 12.

1. Press all the wrinkles out of the background fabric, then stabilize it with lightweight fusible interfacing.
2. Starch all the other fabrics.
3. Using the photograph of the quilt as your guide, audition and draw a row of mountains on the green batik fabric. Cut and glue into place. Repeat with the rose batik, creating a row of rose mountains.

4. Audition, cut, and glue preprinted trees into place. Spend the necessary time to fussy cut tree tops.

Starch the tree fabric heavily or the trees will roll when you cut them.

5. Use the medium purple to add a thin strip of shoreline.
6. To accurately create a mirror image of the reflecting trees, lay a strip of tree fabric, right side down, on top of the trees already on the canvas. Pin to secure. Draw directly onto the fabric strip, creating reflections by mimicking the indentations of the different levels of previously glued trees.
7. Remove the pinned trees. Audition, cut, and glue them into place following the shoreline.
8. Audition, cut, and glue groupings of boulders along the shoreline.
   Optional: Incorporate green dryer lint along the shoreline under the rocks.
9. Place an overlay of the dark turquoise tulle over the water, reflected trees, and half of the moss.
10. Baste the entire composition with invisible thread. Trim excess tulle, as necessary.
11. Steam the canvas from the back. Square the canvas and add stabilized borders.
12. Sandwich your quilt. Add a label. Quilt, block, and square the quilt. Add binding and a sleeve, and you're done!

CHAPTER NINE

Photograph by Valori Wells

Tantalizing Trees

Trees really are the window dressing of our landscapes. Trees add scale and perspective in our landscapes and give us visual clues regarding distance. A beautifully designed tree can be a stunning addition to a landscape quilt and a focal point. In this chapter, I introduce you to a variety of quilts and projects focusing on trees.

Fairytale Wood

Inspiration and Basics

The inspiration for this delightful landscape quilt was a graphic by gifted illustrator Trina Schart Hyman. Mona Hutchinson truly captured the whimsical fairytale atmosphere of the original illustration, using a magical combination of fabrics as her medium. Beginning this charming quilt in a workshop I taught in Sisters, Oregon, Mona caught on quickly and had this quilt designed on the wall in nothing flat. Pleased that she had taken to landscape quilting so quickly, Mona said picking out the colors and design was her favorite part of creating the quilt and that trying this type of quilting has given her more self-confidence.

Making the Fabric Her Own

The beauty of Mona's interpretation relied on her ability to incorporate just the right fabrics into her quilt. Rather than choosing complex fabrics with too many values and elements, Mona kept her design simple, thereby reinforcing the fairytale-like theme. Her choice to *not* add a border for framing was intuitive. Some quilts look better with borders, others don't. This quilt stands beautifully on its own. The thin black and gray lines, created with thread, outline the mountains and foreground trees and further enhance the design.

Fairytale Wood, Mona Hutchinson, Milwaukee, Oregon, 18″ × 38″, 2005, inspired by an illustration by Trina Schart Hyman.

Covered Bridge, Joyce R. Becker, Kent, Washington, 28″ × 27″, 2003, from the collection of Anna L. Fishkin, Red Rooster Fabrics.

Inspiration and Basics

I've always been drawn to covered bridges. A compilation of covered bridge photographs, along with a line of vibrant fall fabrics by Red Rooster Fabrics (see Resources), inspired this quilt. My goal during the design process was to create two focal points: the covered bridge and the large foreground tree. Incorporating focal points at *different* positions within the quilt helped create visual impact and interest.

Making the Fabric My Own

Using all-purpose inks and fabric markers to shade the foreground tree produced dramatic results, causing it to pop against the vibrant fall background fabrics. Extending the tree onto the stabilized borders added another dimension to this quilt.

Materials

- Stabilized muslin canvas: 28″ × 27″
- Sky, light blue-gray fabric: $1/2$ yard
- Sky overlay, white tulle: $1/2$ yard
- Background, muted multicolored fabric, fall colors: $1/2$ yard
- Foothills, vibrant multicolored fabric, fall colors: $1/2$ yard
- Boulders, medium brown fabric: $1/2$ yard
- Ground-cover vegetation, multicolored fabric, fall colors: $1/2$ yard
- Tree/limb, medium to medium-dark bark-like fabric: $1/2$ yard
- Tree leaves, vibrant hand-dyed fabric in fall colors, yellow, orange, red, and green: $1/2$ yard
- Bridge/fence, medium brown weathered board–like fabric: $1/2$ yard
- Roof, medium-dark red roof-like fabric: $1/4$ yard
- Bridge front, black tulle: $1/4$ yard

- Water, sapphire blue fabric with white speckles: $1/4$ yard
- Inner border, medium rust fabric: $3/8$ yard
- Outer border and binding, multicolored bark-like fabric: $3/4$ yard
- Backing and sleeve: $1 1/4$ yards
- Batting: 32″ × 31″
- Lightweight fusible interfacing for canvas and borders
- Spray starch
- Tsukineko All-Purpose Ink: gray, chocolate brown, white, and black
- Fantastix applicators: bullet-tipped and sharp-tipped
- Fabric markers (optional)
- Sea sponge cut into small manageable bits
- Freezer paper
- Threads: invisible, matching, and chartreuse variegated

Cutting

Inner border, mitered: Cut 4 strips $2 1/2$″ × width of fabric.
Outer border, mitered: Cut 4 strips 4″ × width of fabric.
Binding: Cut 3 strips $2 1/2$″ × width of fabric.
Sleeve: Cut 1 strip $8 1/2$″ × width of fabric.

Construction

Refer to Chapters 1, 2, and 5.

1. Follow the instructions for creating a canvas.
2. Audition, cut, and glue the sky fabric to the canvas. Depending on the value of the sky, audition, cut, and pin 1 or 2 layers of white tulle over the sky fabric.
3. Starch all the other fabrics.
4. Audition, cut, position, and glue background and foothill fabrics into place.
5. Audition the vibrant multicolored leaf fabric. Cut small clumps and glue them into place at the base of the foothills.
6. Referring to the photograph of the quilt as your guide, draw a covered bridge onto the dull side of freezer paper for use as a template. Audition the covered bridge template on your canvas, making size adjustments if necessary. Cut apart the freezer paper to create individual templates for the bridge, the bridge front, and the roof.
7. For the bridge and roof, iron the freezer-paper templates, shiny-side down, onto the front side of the selected fabrics. Cut. Pin the bridge front template onto the black tulle and cut. Remove the freezer paper and then glue the individual bridge elements into place on the canvas.
8. Using the same prestarched bridge fabric, cut narrow $1/2$″ rails and fence posts. Position and glue the fence into place.

9. Audition the water fabric on your canvas; cut, position, and glue it into place.
10. Cut individual boulders of different sizes from the boulder fabric. Audition the boulders on top of the water, using smaller boulders in the distance and larger ones in the foreground. Position and glue the boulders into place.
11. Audition ground-cover vegetation (shrubs, grasses, foliage, etc.). Cut, position, and glue the ground cover in place, increasing the scale as you move forward in the landscape.
12. Audition bark-like fabric for the tree and limbs. Cut, position, and glue the tree and limbs into place. Add more ground cover peaking from behind and in front of the tree; glue into place.
13. Cut clumps of leaves from the hand-dyed leaf fabric. Position and glue the leaves into place.
14. Baste the entire composition with invisible thread. Trim excess tulle, as necessary.

Special Effects and Finishing

Refer to Chapters 3, 4, and 12.

1. Place your canvas on a protected wall surface before you begin painting with inks. Add details to the landscape with all-purpose inks and markers. Heat set, as necessary.
   - Shade the bridge, fence rails, and posts with gray, black, and white ink to give the appearance of wooden planks.
   - Add dimension to the bridge roof with black ink and a sharp-tipped applicator.
   - Add swirling foam to the water with white ink and a sharp-tipped applicator.
   - Use inks with applicators and a sea sponge to add shading and dimension to the tree bark.
   - With inks and fabric markers (optional), add shading to the boulders.

Remember to work from the top of the canvas down when using inks or paint so you don't smear your work.

2. Dry and heat set all painted elements, if necessary.
3. Enhance the landscape with free-motion machine embroidery.
   - Use circular stitches and the variegated chartreuse thread to create moss between the boulders.
   - Add branches and twigs to the tree using a matching brown thread.
   - Define and enhance the ground vegetation with matching threads.

- Add definition to leaves by stitching down their centers with matching thread to create veins.
- Machine embroider planks on the bridge and roof with a matching thread.

4. Steam the canvas from the back. Square the canvas and add stabilized borders.
5. Extend the tree trunk, branches, and leaves into the borders. Baste these in place. Add highlights with inks; dry and heat set.
6. Machine embroider additional elements, if desired.
7. Sandwich your quilt. Add a label. Quilt, block, and square the quilt. Add binding and a sleeve, and you're done!

The Easy Version

Instead of adding accents with inks, use a commercial fabric that looks like bubbling, moving water. Use a bridge-like plank fabric instead of painting the bridge with inks. Select a pre-printed commercial roof fabric and use it instead of painting the barn roof. Eliminate the boulders.

Live Oak

Inspiration and Basics

Using photographs she took in the countryside of "beautiful weathered live oaks along the road," Sandy Bosley began her landscape quilt with a simple line drawing. She admits she has been "hooked on landscape quilts" since the 1980s and creates several a year. An accomplished artist, Sandy has appeared on *Simply Quilts,* and her work has been exhibited in national and international exhibits, museums, and quilting magazines. Sandy hand painted the graceful giant oak using textile paints and extended the scene with hand embroidery, raw-edge appliqué, and free-form piecing. She enjoys color selection and blending fabrics, and says she feels good "when fabrics transition one to another smoothly."

Making the Fabric Her Own

Sandy created the sky and foreground using free-form pieced units of commercial, hand-dyed, and hand-painted fabrics that were cut apart then sewn together to create new fabric. She blended the colors with Versatex textile paint (see Resources). Sandy's unique method of free-form piecing allows her to create and integrate commercial and hand-painted fabrics with spectacular results. To achieve continuity in her quilts, Sandy often embellishes with inks, paints, embroidery flosses, and threads.

Live Oak, Sandy Bosley, Bothell, Washington, 45″ × 41″, 2002.

Aspens, Georgia McRae, Gig Harbor, Washington, 34″ × 35″, 2004.

Aspens

Inspiration and Basics

Georgia McRae's colorful landscape pays homage to poignant memories of growing up in the Northeast. Georgia said her biggest challenge was the free-form cutting and placement of the fabrics on the canvas. She says, "Trusting that my quilt would work in terms of perspective, size, and design relationships was difficult, but it worked!" A prize-winning "wearable" artist, Georgia enjoyed the extensive machine embroidery, quilting, and embellishment of her landscape quilt.

Making the Fabric Her Own

Georgia's ability to integrate the background fabrics forms the foundation of this successful quilt. The yellow foliage combined with the gray and blue background fabrics, as well as the smaller aspen trees in the distance, gives this landscape great perspective. The dark markings on the trees combined with the twisted branches also add to the realism, as does the colorful foliage in the foreground.

Morning Mist and Blooms

Inspiration and Basics

Inspired by the desire to create a masterpiece of her own, Ramona McCluskey challenged herself to create a successful landscape quilt. A quilter for many years, Ramona said she knew she hadn't found that "point of passion" that she wanted to experience in quilting until she began working on this landscape quilt. Ramona's goal was to create a scene with a muted, foggy sky, mountains, fir trees, and a colorful meadow filled with wildflowers.

Making the Fabric Her Own

When creating her sky, Ramona manipulated several fabrics to provide dramatic results. From a distance, the sky seems like one integrated fabric with shadows and fog. As you get closer to the design, however, you notice that it is multileveled, with layers of gray fabrics on top of the sky fabric and layers of sheer organza to create the misty, cloudy appearance. Ramona went to great lengths to create her unique trees and found flowers for her meadow that are the perfect scale and value, growing larger near the bottom edge.

Morning Mist and Blooms, Ramona R. McCluskey, Seattle, Washington, 25″ × 27″, 2005.

CHAPTER TEN

Stunning Scenes

In this chapter, we witness the essence of a landscape in the purist sense—where the scene itself becomes the focal point, electrifyingly beautiful. We travel deep into the forest and discover a plethora of wild mushrooms, then we go on to Italy to a bright and sunny villa, and then on to a strenuous hike on a peak in Brazil. Next, we trek through a frosty winter scene, take a stroll in a peaceful garden, and then scale Mount Assiniboine in the Canadian Rockies.

Photograph by Valori Wells

Autumn Magic

Inspiration and Basics

Describing a day of hiking near Upper Kananaskis Lake in Alberta, Kay Gould says, "My husband and I were surprised at the magnificent colors and forms of the more than 30 types of mushrooms we discovered along the trail." Using as inspiration the digital images her husband, Ross, took during their hike, Kay's unique landscape quilt exudes an almost mystical quality, showcasing the unexpected mushrooms growing on the mossy forest floor. Kay says, "I really enjoyed manipulating the fabric colors with Prismacolor and Derwent pencils." Her greatest challenge was creating depth and perspective. To make the mushrooms pop from the background elements, Kay satin stitched the edges of each mushroom. Angelina fibers and tulle highlight the focal mushroom.

Autumn Magic, Kay Gould, Calgary, Alberta, 29˝ × 25˝, 2005.

Making the Fabric Her Own

To create a soft forest floor for her mushrooms, Kay used preprinted fabrics with leaves, pine needles, twigs, and moss.

Kay's uncanny ability to create the individual mushrooms from fabrics she manipulated with paint, artist pencils, folding, overlays, and so on was amazing. It was almost as if she could see the finished mushrooms appear on the fabric *before* she created them!

Old World Charm, Joyce R. Becker, Kent, Washington, 30˝ × 25˝, 2004.

Old World Charm

Inspiration and Basics

In my dreams, I often travel to exotic places. In one dream, my husband and I visit Tuscany, Italy, and maneuver the crooked streets to our destination, a sun-baked villa on top of a hill overlooking a bay. When we arrive, we are ushered to an outdoor piazza where the aroma of roasted garlic and simmering Italian sauces lingers in the air. After a scrumptious feast, we relax on the balcony of our villa, basking in the sun while the balmy breezes caress us. *Old World Charm* puts me in the middle of this dream. Perhaps one day my dream will come true. Using six companion fabrics from Fabri-Quilt's Renoir's Village collection, I let the fabrics do the work as I recreated my "villa in the sun" fantasy. After the fabrics hung on my design wall for a few days, they began to take on their own personality, dictating where they should appear in the landscape.

Making the Fabric My Own

In an effort to make this image appear to be from another time, I strove for an impressionistic feel, with blurry rather than sharp edges. To accomplish that goal, I adjusted the way I machine embroidered, moving the canvas rapidly back and forth rather than using a slower, more controlled stitch. Students enjoy creating their own interpretations of this scene using kits I provide in my *Old World Charm* workshops.

Itatiaia, Annette van Rooij Valtl, Remscheid, Germany, 37″ × 30″, 2004.

Itatiaia

Inspiration and Basics

Saying she always wanted to recreate "the special place" where she first met her husband while climbing in Brazil, Annette van Rooij Valtl created a landscape quilt that pays homage to Itatiaia. Annette says, "The whole process of creating landscapes is pure joy—choosing the best fabrics, shaping, and bringing the quilt alive with embroidery, shading, and quilting." Showing up for my workshop bursting with energy and enthusiasm, Annette was eager to create a successful landscape quilt that pushed beyond the boundaries of traditional quilt making, to "disassociate, or get free, from traditional forms of quilting, stepping onto new land."

Making the Fabric Her Own

One of Annette's best attributes was her ability to stand back from her piece and make adjustments, adding shading with fabric crayons or different values of fabrics when necessary. Using a myriad of fabrics for shading, along with fabric crayons and extensive machine embroidery with colored threads, Annette definitely realized her goal of recreating a "detailed, realistic impression of Itatiaia."

Cabin in the Woods, Joyce R. Becker, Kent, Washington, 55˝× 39˝, 2004.

Cabin in the Woods

Inspiration and Basics

I have always wanted to design and create a scene using only black and white values. When I discovered a commercial fabric with realistic black and white preprinted mountains, it set my creative juices in motion. After creating the background, I used an overlay of bonded white Angelina fiber to make the snowy surface appear frosty and slippery. I placed an overlay of white tulle over the surface of the whole quilt top to integrate the elements.

Making the Fabric My Own

Before placing the overlay of white tulle over the entire quilt, I used gray and white inks to paint in the planks, windows, and doors of the cabin, making it look old and weathered. I framed the landscape quilt with fusible gray bias tape so the viewer would seem to be gazing at a winter scene through a leaded glass window.

Assiniboine Mist

Inspiration and Basics

More often than not, landscape quilts are triggered by fond memories, packed full of emotion and feelings of well-being. Connie Morrison's love affair with Mount Assiniboine, located in the Canadian Rockies, dates back to her honeymoon, when she and her husband backpacked to the mountain. Using an original photograph, Connie's goal was to create a "feeling of majesty, so the viewer would feel what a beautiful, mystical kind of place it is." Allowing herself the freedom to play, Connie cut a variety of whimsical trees and set them on a rocky cliff overlooking the majestic mountain.

Making the Fabric Her Own

Connie had great fun in this workshop, and it was truly inspiring to watch her vision grow. With complete abandonment, she cut and glued, experimenting with a variety of fabrics, textures, and embellishments. Using tulle and shredded Thermore batting, Connie successfully recreated the misty fog creeping across the cliffs on the mountain.

Assiniboine Mist, Connie Morrison, Red Deer, Alberta, 31˝× 41˝, 2005.

Country Garden, Donna Haugan, Lolo, Montana, 32″ × 32″, 2004.

Inspiration and Basics

Totally convinced she would never be able to create a quilt without a pattern, Donna Haugan became a convert when she took my workshop and created this award-winning quilt. Inspired by a card with flowers and birds, Donna turned her landscape into a country garden with lilac bushes and birch trees, alive with colorful butterflies, birds, flowers, and even chickens strolling about in the dappled sunlight. A quilter for more than twenty years, Donna says, "I always wanted to be an artist and didn't think I could. But look at me now—I think I am getting close!" Using a beautiful hand-dyed fabric as the background for this landscape, Donna said her biggest accomplishment in this quilt was "making it look like you could walk into the scene."

Making the Fabric Her Own

While working on this quilt, Donna discovered that she had the ability to manipulate and change things. For example, when the birch trees seemed too stark, she shaded them with black colored pencils. She used overlays for shadowing and dimension and added machine-embroidered butterflies and a whimsical birdhouse for interest.

Materials

- Stabilized muslin canvas: 32″ × 32″
- Sky, multicolored fabric, greens, blues, and yellow with tree motifs: $1/2$ yard
- Fabrics with lilacs, red roses, yellow roses, geraniums, foxgloves, yellow daisies: fat quarter each
- Birch bark–like white fabric: fat quarter
- Birdhouse, brown weathered fabric: $1/4$ yard
- Brick, red fabric: $1/2$ yard

- Fence posts, rails, and gate, gray fabric: fat quarter
- Rooster, hen fabric: $1/4$ yard
- Variety of leaves, foliage, and bushes, green fabrics: fat quarter each
- Basket, yellow basket-weave fabric: $1/4$ yard
- Brick and gatepost overlay, black tulle: $1/4$ yard
- Borders and binding, green leaf fabric: $7/8$ yard
- Backing and sleeve: $1^3/8$ yards
- Batting: 36″ × 36″
- Lightweight fusible interfacing for canvas and borders
- Spray starch
- Fabric markers: black and green
- Artist colored pencils: gray and black
- Threads: invisible, matching, and moss green

Cutting

Borders, mitered: Cut 4 strips $3^1/2$″ × width of fabric.
Binding: Cut 4 strips $2^1/2$″ × width of fabric.
Sleeve: Cut 1 strip $8^1/2$″ × width of fabric.

Construction

Refer to Chapters 1, 2, and 4.

1. Follow the instructions for creating a canvas.
2. Audition, cut, position, and glue the sky fabric onto the canvas.
3. Starch all the other fabrics.
4. Audition, cut, position, and glue elements into place in the following sequence: lilac bushes, birch trees, birdhouse and pole, foxgloves, then brick walkway.
5. Cut and glue fence posts and rails. Then build a gate with fence fabric and glue into place. Cut and glue additional fence posts and rails, if needed.
6. Audition, cut, position, and glue chickens and yellow roses into place.
7. Cut, position, and glue red roses on the fence and growing up the trees.
8. Cut, position, and glue additional foliage, leaves, and bushes into place.
9. Audition, cut, and glue the basket into place. Add geraniums in the basket.
10. Place an overlay of black tulle over the bricks from the gate down for shading.
11. Cut and glue in place a double layer of black tulle to create a shadow effect for the gatepost.
    Optional: Create a garden hat with a ribbon to hang on the fence post.
12. Baste the entire composition with invisible thread. Trim excess tulle, as necessary.

Special Effects and Finishing

Refer to Chapters 3, 4, and 12.

1. Add details to the landscape with fabric markers and colored pencils.
   - Using a black marker, add texture to the birch trees, fence, and fence posts.
   - With a green marker, draw a heart on the garden gate.
   - Use colored pencils to draw planks on the gate and fence posts.
2. Enhance the landscape with free-motion machine embroidery.
   - Using small, circular stitches and moss green thread, embroider moss between the bricks.
   - Create machine-embroidered butterflies and birds on stabilizer; appliqué them onto the canvas.
3. Steam the canvas from the back. Square the canvas and stabilized borders.
4. Sandwich your quilt. Add a label. Quilt, block, and square the quilt. Add binding and a sleeve, and you're done!

The Easy Version

Simplify this quilt by eliminating some of the flowers, such as the lilac bushes. Use preprinted commercial elements for the birdhouse, birds, basket, butterflies, and birch trees.

CHAPTER ELEVEN

Photograph by Valori Wells

Great Gifts and More

What else can you create with your newfound talents? This chapter offers many suggestions, including landscape quilts for kids and quick-and-easy gifts created using digital photographs. How about a landscape photograph with an oil canvas finish, or how about adding Angelina fiber for a new twist? Think about a landscape greeting card or even a fabric bowl with a landscape inspiration... There truly is no limit to your creativity!

The Beauty of Alaska

Landscapes Are for Kids, Too

Inspiration and Basics

No novice to quilting, my granddaughter Shelbie Rose Valdez began creating quilts while in grade school for the annual Reflections competition promoting the arts. When Shelbie entered middle school, she decided it was time to try a landscape quilt. She took a photograph of a hillside in Denali, Alaska, and she says, "It was so beautiful; I decided to make it into a quilt." Her landscape quilt *The Beauty of Alaska* won a first-place ribbon at her school and at the district level, and she went on to the state competition. Digging through my considerable stash until she found fabrics she liked, and using her photograph as inspiration, Shelbie built her canvas from the top down, saying, "I liked cutting and gluing the most." The pièce de résistance was her discovery of a grizzly bear fabric in my stash. Instead of using a traditional binding, Shelbie zigzag stitched around the perimeter of the quilt.

Try not to be overbearing and opinionated when mentoring children's creativity. Praise them and make them feel good about what they've done. Remember, it's their project, not yours!

Making the Fabric Her Own

Although it was tedious, Shelbie actually cut separate flowers resembling the Indian paintbrush flowers that grow wild in Alaska, along with individual bushes and foliage. Shelbie says, "Cutting and quilting all of the leaves, flowers, and grassy hills was my biggest challenge, but I did it!"

The Beauty of Alaska, Shelbie Rose Valdez, Auburn, Washington, 28˝ × 23˝, 2003.

Black Beach, Joyce R. Becker, Kent, Washington, 15″ × 14″, 2003.

Black Beach

Inspiration and Basics

If you're like me, you're always searching for just the right gift for a special occasion. I'm not sure why or how it happens, but most quilters sometimes feel it's not only our duty but also our moral obligation to make and give away our treasured quilts. As a quilter who has made and given away many large heirloom quilts, I'm now all for creating quick-and-easy gifts. Using the same type of framing I might use when designing a landscape quilt, I look for opportunities to capture stunning scenes with my digital camera, incorporating visual interest in the background, middle ground, and foreground. I also consider how to position focal points, include negative space, and keep it simple. Traveling and teaching in New Zealand, my husband and I came across an amazing beach with grayish-black sand.

Begging my husband to "stop *again,*" I jumped out of the car and began snapping digital photographs of the beach. With the random placement of the driftwood on the beach, the stream flowing into the ocean, and the intense blue of the water, it was a scene only God could have created. Using the methods described in Chapter 3, I imported a digital photograph of the black beach into Adobe PhotoDeluxe, enlarged it, enhanced the color and values, and printed it on computer-ready fabric.

Making the Fabric My Own

Embroidering the grassy area in the left corner and carrying that same threadwork into the inner border gave this quilt another point of interest. The directional stitching in the sand, stream, wet sand, and water reinforces the theme. Although my intensions were good, I couldn't bear to part with this quilt, so I gave it to myself!

Sunshine and Shadows, Joyce R. Becker, Kent, Washington, 21˝ × 17˝, 2004.

Inspiration and Basics

One day, while perusing my email, I came across a message from Costco.com. Scrolling down a list of the latest specials, I discovered a listing for printing photographs or portraits with a professional oil canvas finish. "Hmm," I thought to myself, "I wonder if this company would enlarge a landscape photograph and print it on an oil canvas?" I sent in my photograph and payment, and, much to my delight, the picture I got back was sharp and clear, with beautiful colors. Even more amazing, the photograph looked and felt like a real oil canvas. There are many Web-based businesses that specialize in enlarging and printing photographs on oil canvas. In most cases, you can mail your photograph, or email a digital image, and have it enlarged, printed on an oil canvas, and returned to you by mail (see Resources). My cost was around $50 to have a standard snapshot enlarged to 14˝ × 11˝ and printed on an oil canvas. Some businesses offer to stretch your canvas on a wooden frame. Another option is to print your own photograph on Gloss Finish Artist Canvas by Vintage Workshop (see Resources). The company offers 8½˝ × 11˝ fabric sheets.

Making the Fabric My Own

Giving myself permission to try something new and *make the fabric my own* by having it printed on oil canvas was a bit scary at first. But as my design developed, I was able to stitch through the canvas and create a landscape quilt. I was elated! There is nothing more satisfying than having a great idea succeed.

Materials

- Enlarged photograph, printed on canvas: 14″ × 11″
- Borders and binding, hand-dyed pastel fabric: ⅝ yard
- Backing and sleeve: 1 yard
- Batting: 25″ × 21″
- Lightweight fusible interfacing for canvas and borders
- Spray starch
- Threads: invisible, variegated, and 30-weight cotton matching machine embroidery
- Jeans needles

Cutting

Border: Cut 3 strips 3½″ × width of fabric.
Binding: Cut 3 strips 2½″ × width of fabric.
Sleeve: Cut 1 strip 8½″ × width of fabric.

Construction

Refer to Chapters 3 and 12.

1. Stabilize your borders until they are the same density or thickness as the oil canvas.
2. Stitch the reinforced borders to the squared oil canvas photograph.

Since the canvas is very thick, consider skipping any machine embroidery and machine quilt instead.

3. Press the borders with a pressing cloth.

Do not place the iron on the oil canvas; it will melt.

4. Sandwich your quilt and add a label.
5. Machine quilt, using a jeans needle and specialty threads.
   - Use small, circular quilting stitches and a matching variegated thread for the flower blossoms.
   - Create foliage between the flower blossoms, using a circular stitch and a variegated chartreuse thread.
   - Using several values of thread and a small side-to-side stitch, create texture and shading on the garden columns.
   - To create depth and shadow in this scene, use darker threads in the distance and brighter threads as you move forward.
   - Stipple quilt the borders, following the shadows and dappled sunlight effects of the fabric.
6. Because the canvas is rigid, you don't have to block this quilt.
7. Square the quilt. Add binding and a sleeve, and you're done!

Bellows Beach

Inspiration and Basics

Created specifically for the annual faculty auction at the International Quilt Festival in Houston, Texas, in 2004, *Bellows Beach* was really quick and fun project that allowed me some creative freedom. Using a digital photograph I took at Bellows Beach, in Oahu, Hawaii, I manipulated the image in a photo program and printed it on computer-ready fabric. After the photo was heat set, it was stabilized with *two* layers of fusible stabilizer. The shaggy ironwood tree was embroidered with thick cotton thread to add extra needles and bulk to the tree.

Making the Fabric My Own

Adding an overlay of Angelina on the water added sparkle and a touch of whimsy to this quilt. The textural threadwork on the pine needles makes the ironwood tree a focal point.

Materials

- Pretreated computer fabric, white: 1 sheet (8½″ × 11″)
- Border and binding, aqua blue batik: ⅞ yard
- Backing and sleeve: ⅞ yard
- Batting: 20″ × 18″
- Lightweight fusible interfacing for printed photograph and borders
- Spray starch
- Angelina fibers: Mint Sparkle
- Threads: invisible and matching

Cutting

Borders, mitered: Cut 4 strips 4½″ × width of fabric.
Binding: Cut 3 strips 2½″ × width of fabric.
Sleeve: Cut 1 strip 8½″ × width of fabric.

Bellows Beach, Joyce R. Becker, Kent, Washington, 16″× 14″, 2004. Photograph courtesy of Ken Wagner.

Construction

Refer to Chapters 1, 3, and 12.

1. Print the photograph on the pretreated computer fabric and then square the image.
2. Stabilize the photograph with 2 layers of fusible stabilizer.
3. Stabilize the borders and add them to the quilt top.
4. Press the top with a pressing cloth.

Special Effects and Finishing

Refer to Chapters 4 and 12.

1. Enhance the landscape with free-motion machine embroidery.

■ Embroider shaggy needles onto the ironwood tree, using at least 2 thread values.

■ Add crevices onto the mountains with a matching thread.

■ Using a matching thread and an elongated stitch, embroider the sky.

2. Bond Angelina fibers and glue them into place over the water. Baste the fibers into place with invisible thread.
3. Sandwich your quilt. Add a label. Quilt, block, and square the quilt. Add binding and a sleeve, and you're done!

A Greeting Card Landscape,
Barbara Szijarto, Edmonton,
Alberta, 4″ × 6″, 2005.

A Greeting Card Landscape

Inspiration and Basics

After reading *Luscious Landscapes,* Barbara Szijarto sent me digital photographs of her one-of-a-kind, whimsical landscape greeting cards. Dubbing herself "The Queen Gnome and President of the World-Wide Gnome Association," Barbara says, "I love working with gnomes because of my passion for nature and gardening." Her vision for this card depicts a female gnome heading out of her studio to purchase *Beautifully Embellished Landscapes.* Barbara began with a starched muslin background, auditioned her background fabrics, made pattern pieces, and added elements in logical order until she was sure of the order. Next, she glued or bonded the elements into place and stitched them with a variety of straight, zigzag, and embroidery stitches. Barbara drew, digitized, and machine embroidered the gnome in the foreground, using a hoop and her embroidery machine, and then framed the landscape with borders made of embroidered card stock.

Barbara loves shopping for fabrics, especially checking out used clothing shops. After she brings the fabrics home, she washes and starches them before adding them to her collection.

Making the Fabric Her Own

When asked why she enjoys making her distinctive greeting cards, Barbara said, "The greatest thing about making greeting cards is that they can be created with lots of recycled materials. These cards combine many crafts and are a bridge between scrapbooking, sewing, and quilting. You are limited only by your imagination, and that's limitless!"

Pieceful Garden Bowl

Inspiration and Basics

Sonia Grasvik is one of those talented people who can translate what they see in their mind's eye into reality. Sonia says, "I allow my whimsical, playful side to show up when I create my bowls." Calling herself a "passionate quilt artist," Sonia says she enjoys playing with new ideas. The quilted bowls she designs and creates began as a simple challenge to see whether she could work out the construction methodology. Sonia says, "The bowls serve as a fun and quick project when I am between quilts, and they satisfy my love of embellishment." Using Sonia's bowl pattern (see Resources), create a bowl similar to Sonia's. Use fabrics that resemble a garden wall. If desired, include climbing vines made from painted jute and appliqué them into place with invisible thread.

Making the Fabric Her Own

To create the flowers, try Sonia's method: Sandwich 2 layers of white tulle in a stretched hoop. Create French knots, by hand, with perle cotton for the flowers and leaves. Cut away the tulle and appliqué the flowers and leaves onto the bowl with invisible thread. Incorporate found objects into your design for visual interest, depth, and scale.

Problem Solving

The secret to successful landscape quilts lies in your ability to keep trying. When one method doesn't work, try something else. If that doesn't work, think about simplifying. Sometimes, we need to stand back from our work and just let it percolate inside our heads for a while. Sometimes answers to problems arrive in the form of a dream. Going around a roadblock instead of through it, we can sometimes achieve our goal by approaching from another direction. Trust your instinct and intuitive nature. You'll eventually find a solution to your dilemma.

Chapter 12 leads you into the final phase of finishing your landscape quilt. Don't skip these steps; they are extremely important.

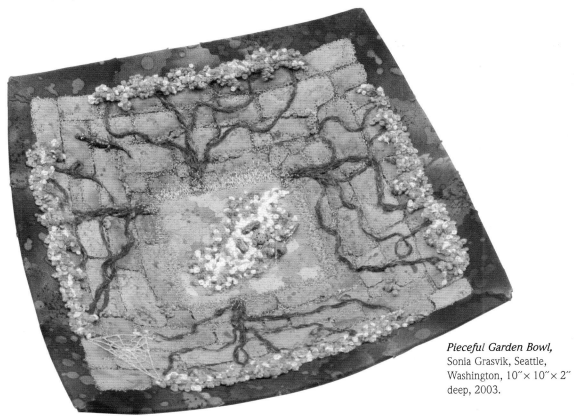

Pieceful Garden Bowl,
Sonia Grasvik, Seattle,
Washington, 10″ × 10″ × 2″
deep, 2003.

Faultless Finishing

It's funny how we change over the years. Twenty years ago, when I made mostly traditional quilts, my philosophy when it came to mistakes was "It'll quilt out" or "Nobody will notice if my blocks aren't quite square when the quilt is on the bed." I wasn't concerned about perfection or the details that go into creating well-executed, award-winning quilts. When I began creating landscape quilts, my philosophy did an about-face. I discovered that it *does* matter whether your quilt top is square before you put on the borders, and that quilts with mitered bindings and straight borders look better than quilts with rippled edges. In fact, uneven or rippled edges actually distract the eye from the beauty of the quilt. It really began to bother me when I saw quilts hanging in a show that were messy, with thread tails dangling, or that were covered in pet hair. At some point, I guess it just hit me: my quilts deserve better. If I'm going to put a considerable amount of time and energy into creating a beautiful landscape quilt,

then the quilt deserves the same amount of attention when it comes to the finishing details.

In this chapter, I present you with the finishing methods necessary to ensure that your landscape quilts hang beautifully on the wall.

Summer Sizzle, Rosellen Carolan, Auburn, Washington, 17″× 15″, 2004, from a workshop with Melody Crust.

Pressing Your Landscape Quilt Top

You've finished your landscape quilt top. You are so excited you can hardly wait until it's quilted and hanging on the wall. Well, take a deep breath and put on the brakes. Before you go any further, there are a few more steps to take. First, you need to press your quilt top *from the back* with *lots of steam*.

If you've forgotten to heat set all your surface-design work—such as painting—you need to go back a step and heat set your quilt top, from the back, with a pressing cloth (Chapter 3). If you skip this step, the colors might bleed.

Once you've heat set everything, go ahead and iron the back of your quilt top *aggressively*, working out all the little puckers and wrinkles with the steam.

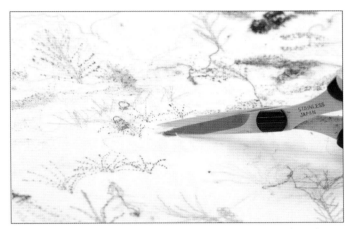

Release a pucker by snipping through the muslin canvas, *not* through the fabrics.

If you come across a pucker that won't steam out, feel free to "release it" using your sharp embroidery scissors. Snip from the back through the muslin canvas *only*, not through the fabrics on the quilt top.

Squaring Your Quilt Top

Once your quilt top has been steam pressed, it's time to square it.

1. Place your quilt top on your gridded cutting mat.
2. Using the printed lines on your mat as your guide, line up your quilt top on the mat so it is square and straight.

If your landscape quilt includes a horizontal water line, take extra precautions when squaring your quilt to make sure that the horizon line is parallel to the top and bottom edges of the quilt top. (See Water on page 36.)

3. Using a straight-edge acrylic ruler and rotary cutter, trim one side of your quilt so it is straight.
4. Place the ruler on the bottom edge corner. Trim.
5. Place the ruler on the upper edge corner. Trim the side, then the upper edge.
6. Repeat the process on the opposite side of the quilt.

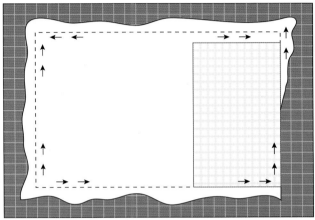

Square the sides, then the top and bottom of each corner.

7. Measure your quilt top in several locations, horizontally and vertically. If the measurements are off, trim as necessary. Measure diagonally; trim as necessary to square quilt.

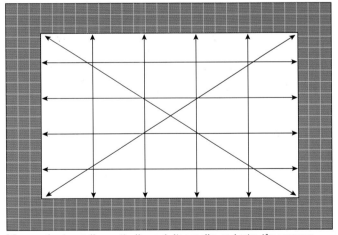

Measure horizontally, vertically, and diagonally, and trim if necessary.

Borders

Only you can decide whether your landscape quilt needs borders. To help you with that decision, I suggest you hang your quilt top canvas on your design wall and look at it for a few days. Do you think the quilt stands on its own, or do you think some framing borders might set it off nicely? If your heart says,

"No, this quilt is lovely on its own and a border would be distracting," then don't add borders. If you are unsure, or if you think a border might enhance your landscape, then by all means, grab your canvas and head to the fabric store to shop for border fabrics.

Although you might *think* you have the perfect border fabric in your stash, in all probability you don't. Border fabrics are tricky. They need to enhance without being overbearing or too stark. Border fabrics need to have movement and include several values. Usually, if you select a border fabric that is one value darker than the darkest value in your quilt, it will work. But which color? Often, if you pick an accent color in your quilt and it's the right value, it will work.

Find a bright, sunny spot in the quilt shop and start pulling bolts of fabric that you think might work as a border fabric. Unroll some of the bolts and place the fabrics you are auditioning next to the quilt top and then look from a distance. Eventually, a fabric will speak to you. If one doesn't, jump in your car and visit a few more shops until you find the perfect fabric.

Pay attention to value when selecting borders. If you select a border fabric with the same value as fabrics in your landscape quilt, you won't have well-defined edges.

Inner and Outer Borders

In a larger landscape quilt, it is sometimes nice to add a narrow inner border in an accent color to "stop the action" of the quilt. This inner border gives the eye a visual clue that the landscape scene has stopped. I particularly favor a 1″ finished inner borders in combination with an outer border that measures from 3″–4½″. I stitch the borders together first and then stitch them to the quilt.

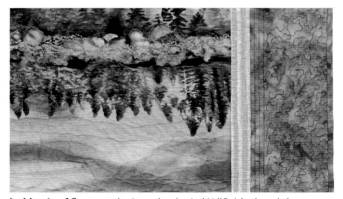

In *Moods of Summer,* the inner border is 1½″ finished, and the outer border is 3½″ finished.

Stitch inner and outer borders together before sewing onto quilt top.

Mitered Borders Without the Work

In keeping with my instant gratification philosophy, I use a simple method I've developed that creates mitered borders without all the work.

1. Stitch all the borders onto the quilt, stopping ¼″ from each corner. At the corner, fold one side to create a 45° angle.

Fold to create a 45° angle.

2. Finger-press the fold line and check the angle with a ruler.
3. Press the fold line with a dry iron.
4. Flip back the folded angle, spray it with repositionable adhesive on a protected surface, and press it into place with a dry iron.

Spray with adhesive.

5. Using a matching or invisible thread and a blind hem stitch, stitch along the fold line.

6. Trim the diagonal seam to $\frac{1}{4}''$. Repeat for each corner.

Stabilizing Borders

A couple of years ago, it occurred to me that my quilt borders should be the same density or thickness as my finished canvas. It was one of those "Duh!" moments. It just made so much sense, I couldn't figure out why I hadn't thought of it sooner. Since that time, I have reinforced my borders with the same fusible interfacing I use on my canvas. Depending on the thickness of my canvas, I use at least one, and sometimes two or three, layers to stabilize my borders.

Because I don't want the extra thickness of the interfacing in my seam allowance, I wait to stabilize my borders until after they are stitched onto the quilt top. After my borders are stitched on and mitered, I butt the interfacing next to the seam allowance and fuse it into place.

Stabilize the borders with interfacing after they are stitched to the quilt top.

Sandwiching Without the Work

As I get older and my old bones get creakier, I find it increasingly difficult to baste my sandwiched quilts on the floor. My smaller quilts are now basted on protected tabletops, and larger quilts on my low-loft carpeted floor. Gone are the days when I crawled around hand basting with a needle and thread or safety pins. Instead, I baste all my quilts with my trusty repositionable spray adhesive.

If you are basting on a tabletop, follow these steps:

1. Cut backing and batting at least 2″ larger on all sides than the squared quilt top.

2. Place a protective layer of plastic on your work surface and place your backing fabric on the protected surface.

3. Place your batting on top of the backing fabric. Fold back half of the batting.

I highly recommend Hobbs Thermore batting (see Resources) for landscape quilts. It is the perfect density, and your quilts will hang straight and flat on the wall.

4. Spray repositionable adhesive on the exposed half of the underside of the batting. Replace the batting and smooth the layers together. Repeat on the other half of the batting.

5. Place the quilt top on top of this sandwich. Fold back the top half of the quilt top, and spray the batting with adhesive. Replace the quilt top and smooth the layers together. Repeat on the other half of the batting.

Spraying adhesive directly onto your quilt top or backing *might* result in spotting or overspray. It's safer to spray the batting.

6. Smooth out any remaining wrinkles on the top and backing of the sandwich.

Labels Without the Work

Your sandwiched quilt is almost ready for machine quilting, except for one important step—adding a label. Since our quilts reflect who we are, the labels on our quilts should also convey that enthusiasm and uniqueness. My method for creating labels is quick and easy. Having a quilt stolen is a life-changing event. After one of my quilts was stolen, I decided to make it next to impossible for anyone to remove a label from one of my quilts. My labels are attached to my quilts during the machine-quilting stage now, making them tough to remove.

STEPS FOR CREATING A LABEL

1. Scan or take a digital photograph of your quilt top or part of your quilt top.

2. Import the photograph into your photo-editing software. Enhance the values and color contrast, if necessary.

3. Add text, including the title of your quilt, your name, where the quilt was made, the size, the date, and if it's a gift, who it's for.

4. Print the label on pretreated computer fabric. Heat set according to the manufacturer's directions.

5. Fold under the edges and press with a pressing cloth; baste the label to the back of your quilt.

When you machine quilt over the label, place invisible thread in your bobbin instead of colored thread.

Machine Quilting

Many of my students have a hard time believing I machine quilt all of my landscape quilts on my home Bernina sewing machines; but I do! At present, I stitch with a Bernina Aurora 440QE with the amazing new free-motion stitch regulator. I also use my Bernina 1080. I'd like to share with you how I machine quilt my landscapes, making it easier for you to comprehend the techniques and try them out yourself.

Equipment

■ Of utmost importance is a good sturdy sewing table, with room to manipulate the quilt during stitching.

My studio setup

■ A true-color lamp with optional magnifying glass helps prevent eyestrain.
■ When you machine quilt, it is important to support the quilt equally on all sides. I often open the drawers on my sewing table to support the weight of my quilt while I machine quilt. If you don't have drawers, consider placing your ironing board at sewing-table height next to your sewing table.

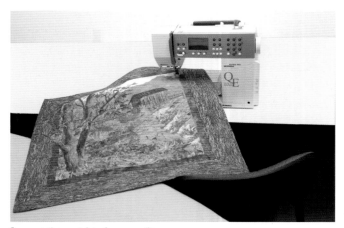

Support the weight of your quilt.

■ Purchase a good-quality office chair and adjust it to the correct ergonomic height for you and your table. Your arms should rest comfortably at a 90° angle to your table.
■ Sit up straight in your chair and scoot yourself as close as possible to your sewing table.
■ Roll your shoulders back and breathe when you stitch. Don't hold your breath or lean forward—that's how you strain your neck, shoulders, and back.

Machine-Quilting Techniques

Machine quilting is the crowning touch on our landscape quilts. My philosophy is that our landscape quilts deserve to be machine quilted with beautiful threads. The extent and depth of machine quilting in your landscape quilt are personal decisions. You can quilt as much or as little as you wish. Here are some suggestions to make your machine quilting go smoothly:

1. Use equal-weight thread on the top and in the bobbin (see page 29).
2. Place your free-motion foot on your machine. Lower the feed dogs and stitch in the needle-down position.
3. Do a test run on a fabric sandwich of equal weight each time you change threads.
4. Change thread colors on the top to match specific elements. Use matching threads if you want background elements to recede.
5. Check the back of your work frequently to make sure your tension is correct and there are no knots, skipped stitches, and so on.
6. Clean out your bobbin area with a brush to prevent lint buildup. Change your needle every time you fill your bobbin.

When I mention changing needles this frequently, my students often look at me like I'm crazy. As needles wear, the holes become larger in your quilt, the shaft becomes dull or rough, and your thread breaks, tangles, or just won't cooperate. It's called preventive maintenance!

7. Quilt with the same density or amount of stitching throughout your quilt so it will hang evenly.
8. Allow the individual elements from nature to dictate your stitching direction or motifs. It is perfectly acceptable to quilt directly over areas that were machine embroidered.
9. If you have difficulty with a particular thread, try changing your needle or adjusting your tension on the top and bottom. If that doesn't work, try a different thread. If all else fails, use an invisible thread.
10. Get up and walk around; stretch every hour.

11. To set off your quilts, or frame them like a piece of art, machine quilt 3 straight lines around your outside border, $1/4"$ apart.

Frame border with 3 rows of quilting.

Framing your quilts, as shown on *Old World Charm*

The Magic of Blocking

Without a doubt, blocking is the most important technique in ensuring that your quilt will hang straight, without unsightly wobbles or rippling edges. Blocking marries the three layers of the quilt together into a cohesive unit. Contributing artist Sonia Grasvik taught me how to block quilts; this knowledge enables me to hang my quilts so that they are straight and square. I have tweaked her methods to fit my needs, and the instructions follow.

Blocking can be done on a low-loft carpet or foam-core board. If you don't have low-loft carpet in your home, consider blocking your quilt at your local quilt shop classroom or in the community room at the library. Or purchase a small carpet remnant just for this purpose. Block your quilt in an out-of-the-way place, where there is little foot or animal traffic!

Blocking Instructions

1. Place a vinyl, flannel-backed tablecloth, vinyl side down, on your carpet or board.
2. Place another absorbent layer of fabric, such as a flat cotton sheet, on top of the tablecloth.
3. Place your quilt, face down, on this sandwich. Pin it into place with T-pins.
4. Fill a small bucket with water.
5. Cut a $10" \times 10"$ square of clean muslin for a pressing cloth, or use a tea towel.
6. Place your iron on a medium-hot setting, with no steam.
7. Dip the muslin pressing cloth into the bucket and moisten it until it is wet but not dripping.
8. Place the wet cloth on one corner of the quilt. Glide the iron across the cloth until it is dry.
9. Rewet the cloth and continue across the surface of the quilt until all areas of the quilt have been blocked.
10. Your quilt needs to remain in this position until it is thoroughly dry. Depending on the weather, it could take hours, or it might not be dry until the next day. To help speed drying, open the windows (weather permitting) and turn on fans.

Squaring Once Again

Although your quilt was squared earlier, you must square it again after you block it. Most of the time, your quilt will not require much trimming. When squaring again, try not to disturb the angle of the mitered corners. Make necessary corrections elsewhere.

Binding

Use your favorite method of binding. I recommend a self-binding—that is, a binding that is the same fabric as your outer border. If your quilt has no borders, use a fabric value that enhances your quilt without blending into it. I recommend a $2 1/2"$-wide straight-grained, double-fold binding.

Sleeve

There are many methods of applying sleeves. I make a fabric tube from an $8 1/2"$ strip of fabric and attach it approximately $1/2"$ below the top edge of the back of the quilt.

Faultless Finishing

At this point, most people would think, "Wow, I'm done." Not me. Remember when I mentioned how quilts hanging in exhibits with thread tails and knots and pet hair really bother me? The last thing you should do to prepare your quilt for hanging is to take care of the finishing details. Put on your spectacles and begin a careful examination of your quilt, snipping thread tails and getting rid of unsightly knots and skipped stitches and anything else that distracts from the beauty of your quilt front and back. Trim back any remaining raw edges on the landscape elements.

Next, hang your quilt over the edge of a table and place a floor lamp nearby so you can see all those pokey invisible thread tails sticking straight out. Carefully snip them off with your sharp embroidery scissors, on both front and back. Place your quilt on a tabletop and go to town with a sticky roller, removing all traces of lint and fuzz, front and back. Last, but not least, wrap two or three layers of duct or masking tape around your hand and go over the entire surface of the quilt, front and back, to remove any other tidbits of materials that don't belong.

Landscape quilts are meant to be displayed on the wall. Because they are not used on the bed, landscape quilts don't need to be laundered. Frankly, I'm not sure what would happen to one of my landscape quilts if I washed it. When your landscape quilt gets dusty, take it outside and give it a good shake. To vacuum, place a layer of netting over the quilt and weigh the netting down; then vacuum the quilt with an upholstery attachment.

Storing and Shipping

As you'll soon discover, landscape quilts do not like to be folded. Creases can remain if a quilt is folded for long periods of time. Rather than folding your landscape quilts for storing or shipping, consider rolling them on a protected tube or a swimming noodle. Roll so the front of the quilt faces *out*. Another option for shipping is to place your quilt in a box and place crumpled acid-free tissue under the fold lines. Store your rolled quilts in a cotton bag or sheet, *not in plastic*. If you have a guest bed, store your quilts flat on the bed and cover them with a cotton sheet.

Conclusion

I think it's fitting that I conclude this book with a "Joyceism." It's my philosophy in quilting and in everyday life. I hope it will inspire you to take chances in your life and with your quilting endeavors. Here goes: Failure leads to discovery. Discovery leads to creation. Creation leads to one-of-a-kind works of art (or in life, new roads to travel).

Thank you for allowing me the opportunity to share my work and methods with you. It fills my heart with joy when I am able to see the landscape quilts created as a result of what you've learned in my books. Please feel free to contact me at JBecker3@hotmail.com. My website, www.joycerbecker.com, has a gallery of quilts and booking information.

Resources

505 Spray and Fix temporary repositionable fabric adhesive, J.T. Trading Corporation, www.sprayandfix.com, info@sprayandfix.com

Angelina fiber, Textura Trading Company, www.texturatrading.com

Artfabrik by Laura Wasilowski, www.artfabrik.com, laura@artfabrik.com

Bernina Aurora 440 QE with stitch regulator, by Bernina of America, www.berninausa.com, available at Bernina dealers

Bowl patterns by Sonia Grasvik, SGrasvik@hotmail.com

Computer fabric sheets: Printed Treasures fabric sheets by Milliken, freezer paper sheets, Bubble Jet Set 2000, and June Taylor fabric sheets, available at most quilt shops; Miracle Fabric Sheets, available from Caryl Bryer Fallert at www.bryerpatch.com or from www.softexpressions.com

Derwent watercolor pencils, available at www.Dickblick.com

Dissolve-4X heavy-duty water soluble stabilizer, available at www.superiorthreads.com or at many quilt shops

Fiskars Softouch scissors, Model 9911-7097, available at most quilt shops and www.fiskars.com

Goo Gone, available at Michaels

Hand-dyed fabrics: Just Imagination Hand-Dyed Fabrics by Judy, www.justimagination.com, judy@justimagination.com

Heat Away Thermogauze stabilizer, available at MeinkeToy, www.meinketoy.com

Hobbs Thermore batting, available at most quilt shops or at www.hobbsbondedfibers.com

Julia Laylander landscape artist and fabrics, www.fabricofnature.com

Mickey Lawler's Skydyes, PO Box 370116, West Hartford, CT 06137-0116, www.skydyes.com, available online

Pellon lightweight fusible interfacing, available at most quilt and fabric shops, www.shoppellon.com

Perfect Pearls embossing powder by Julia Andrus, available at Michaels

Photo and clip-art software, available at OfficeMax, www.officemax.com

Printing photos on canvas: www.qualitycanvasphotos.com, www.fromphotostocanvasprints.com, www.canvasprinters.com

Printing photos on canvas with your own printer: Gloss Finish Artist Canvas by Vintage Workshop, www.softexpressions.com

Prismacolor artist pencils, available at Michaels and Discount Art Supplies, www.discountart.com

Red Rooster Fabrics, available at most quilt shops

Reducing glasses, available through Ginger's Needleworks & Quilting, www.quiltknit.com, or at most quilt shops

Shiva Artist's Paintstiks, available at Art Supplies @ Wholesale Prices, www.hofcraft.com

Sulky threads, cotton Blendables, UltraTwist, polyester, Sulky Solvy, Sulky Super Solvy, and Heat Away stabilizers, available at www.sulky.com or at most quilt shops

Superior Threads, The Bottom Line, Rainbows variegated, www.superiorthreads.com; additional threads available at your local quilt and sewing machine shops

Textile paints: Createx, Jacquard, Setacolor, Versatex, and Lumiere textile paints, available at Dharma Trading Company, www.dharmatrading.com

Threads: See Sulky and Superior Threads; additional threads available at your local quilt and sewing machine shops

Tsukineko All-Purpose Ink, Fabrico markers, VersaCraft stamp pads, www.tsukineko.com

Wonder Invisible Thread, Lingerie and Bobbin Thread, YLI Corporation, www.ylicorp.com

Bibliography

Becker, Joyce R., *Luscious Landscapes*, C&T Publishing: Lafayette, CA, 2003.

Colvin, Joan, *Nature's Studio: A Quilter's Guide to Playing With Fabrics and Techniques*, C&T Publishing: Lafayette, CA, 2005.

Johansen, Linda, *Fast, Fun & Easy Fabric Bowls*, C&T Publishing: Lafayette, CA, 2003.

Midgelow-Marsden, Alysn, in conjunction with Vua Arthur of Art Van Go, *Between the Sheets With Angelina: A Workbook for Fusible Fibres*, word4word: Evesham, England 2003, available at www.texturatrading.com.

Powell, William F., *Drawing Trees*, Walter Foster Publishing: Laguna Hills, CA, 2003.

Prince, Nancy, *Simple Thread Painting*, American Quilter's Society: Paducah, KY, 2004.

Rymer, Cyndy Lyle, and the Hewlett-Packard Company, *Photo Fun*, C&T Publishing: Lafayette, CA, 2004.

Rymer, Cyndy Lyle, and Lynn Koolish with the Hewlett-Packard Company, *More Photo Fun*, C&T Publishing: Lafayette, CA, 2005.

Trees & Leaves, Dover Publications permission-free, Mineola, New York, available at www.doverpublications.com.

About the Author

Although she threatens to "settle down one of these days" and write a "spicy" novel, Joyce continues to travel around the globe, teaching and lecturing about landscape quiltmaking. Joyce has appeared on *M'Liss's World of Quilts*, with C&T author and well-known quilting personality M'Liss Rae Hawley, and on *Simply Quilts*. She also co-hosted a promotional DVD for The Tsukineko Company. Joyce enjoys teaching at large conferences, such as the annual International Quilt Festival in Houston, Texas, and she continues to create award-winning landscape quilts. One of the founders of the Association of Pacific Northwest Quilters and the Pacific Northwest Quiltfest, Joyce volunteers for this organization and contributes quilts to its traveling exhibits.

Joyce and her husband, Donald, have a "blended" family and enjoy family get-togethers. When she's not writing, teaching, traveling, or stitching, Joyce enjoys reading, taking walks with her husband, watching the birds gather at the feeders, and hanging out with her quilting friends.

Index

Great Titles
from

C&T PUBLISHING

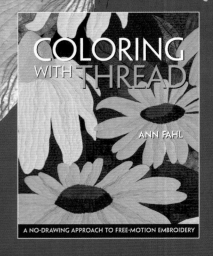

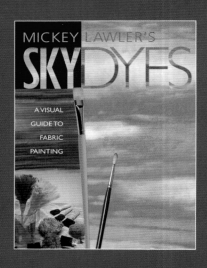
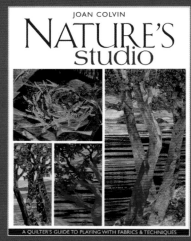
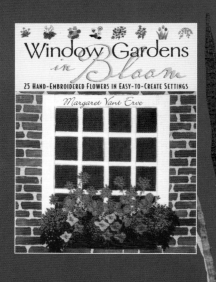